The Ultimate Guide to
CAT BREEDS

THE ULTIMATE GUIDE TO
CAT BREEDS

LOUISA SOMERVILLE

CHARTWELL
BOOKS, INC.

This edition published in 2008 by
CHARTWELL BOOKS, INC.
A division of BOOK SALES, INC.
114 Northfield Avenue
Edison, New Jersey 08837
USA

For all editorial enquiries please contact
Regency House Publishing Ltd at

www.regencyhousepublishing.com

ISBN 13: 978-0-7858-2264-6
ISBN 10: 0-7858-2264-X

Printed in China
by Sino Publishing House Ltd.

All photographs are supplied by kind permission of the
RSPCA Photo Library, with the exception of the
following which are courtesy of **Cogis**: Pages 13, 23, 52,
101 right, 116, 117, 119 right, 128, 147, 158, 161, 178,
179, 203, 204, 206, 207, 213, 216, 228 left, 263 left, 264
both, 266, 267, 276 both, 280, 281, 282, 284, 292, 294,
298, 299, 300, 301, 320 right, 348, 354, 355, 366
Hermeline/Cogis; pages 17 left, 48, 62 right above, 76,
120, 122, 123, 126 left, 129, 132, 133, 134, 135, 136,
137, 174, 215, 220, 222, 233, 234, 236 both, 241, 234,
245, 246, 247, 250 top, 252, 253, 254, 255, 271, 295,
297, 305, 316, 320, 325, 327, 329, 356, 357, 358, 359,
360, 361, 362, 363, 364, Français/Cogis; pages 17
right,18 right, 46, 66, 67, 70, 74, 77, 78, 94, 95, 96, 97,
102, 103, 104, 105, 107, 108, 125, 126 right, 127, 142,
143, 144, 145, 146 left, 157, 163, 168, 181, 183 left,
188, 201, 202, 205, 212, 221, 224, 225, 226, 227, 230,
238, 239, 240 both, 242, 244, 268 left, 272, 273, 274
below, 275, 277, 278, 285, 302, 304, 307, 310, 319, 344,
345 Lanceau/Cogis; pages 45, 47, 49, 75, 151, 176, 187,
232, 308, 322, 329, 330, 338, 339, 340, 341, 347, 350,
351, 353, 370, 371, 375 Excalibur/Cogis; pages 53, 109,
112, 113, 140, 141, 196, 197, 198, 214, 291, 331, 327,
342 Gauzargue/Cogis; pages 54, 56, 57, 62 left and right
below, 82, 83, 148, 149, 150, 160, 169, 172, 173, 177,
185, 199, 208, 209, 218, 219, 228 right, 229, 248, 250
below and right, 251, 265, 270, 279, 283, 286, 287
Labat/Cogis; page 63, 180 Damman/Cogis; pages 166,
336, 337 Labat/Lanceau/Cogis; pages 119 left, 121, 313,
314 right, 317, 346, 349, 352, 373, 374 Schwartz/Cogis;
pages 365, 367, 368 Gelhar/Cogis; page 369
Bernie/Cogis; pages 159, 217, 306 right, 311
Vedie/Cogis; page 237 Gissey/Cogis; Page 269
Zizola/Cogis; page 274 top Rocher/Cogis.

CONTENTS

INTRODUCTION

Cats have been domesticated since prehistoric times, perhaps for as long as 5,000 years. Throughout human history, they have been greatly valued as destroyers of vermin, as well as for their ornamental qualities. However, considering our long and successful relationship with the domestic feline, the phenomenon of the pure-bred cat is a surprisingly recent one.

How many breeds of cats could you identify? The chances are that you might recognize at least a few of the following: Persian, Maine Coon, Siamese, Abyssinian, Russian Blue, Tonkinese, Burmese. These are, in fact, just a few of

OPPOSITE LEFT
Perhaps the most instantly recognizable cat breed of all, the Siamese originated in south-east Asia over 500 years ago.

RIGHT
The Maine Coon is one of the oldest natural breeds in North America and has been recognized as a true variety for well over 100 years. The breed originated in the state of Maine on the north-eastern side of the USA.

LEFT
The Scottish Wildcat has a dense coat, assuring its survival through the harsh Scottish winters, and providing excellent camouflage. This, coupled with its timidity, makes it very difficult to spot. The small wildcats which appear all over the world are the closest relations to our domestic breeds.

Wild cats, such as tigers and pumas, are near relations of today's domestic cats, much of their behaviour being discernible in our fireside friends.

the 40 or so breeds recognized by the world's major cat registries. There are a handful more that are quite new or rare and not yet officially recognized by many feline associations.

Cats have graced us with their presence since the time of the ancient Egyptians, possibly much earlier. But it took the rise in popularity of cat shows in late 19th-century England to kick-start the selective breeding of the domestic cat into separate types. All but a few domestic cat breeds are less than 100 years old, and most of them appeared on the scene far more recently. Compare this to the dog world, where rudimentary selective breeding started several thousand years ago.

A TIGER IN THE HOUSE
The domestic cat is related to lions, tigers, pumas and other wild cats and the similarity in looks and behaviour is imediately apparent. However, it is the smaller wildcat which is the cat's closest relative. The Scottish Wildcat is a fine example and its superb natural camouflage enables it to merge imperceptibly into the surrounding countryside. It is adaptable, hardy and extremely timid. Further south lives the Jungle Cat which, despite its name, inhabits the sandy desert regions of Egypt and has a beautifully ticked coat

which blends in splendidly with the surrounding terrain. There are many other wildcats in evidence throughout the world, but due to extreme timidity, little is unfortunately known about them. In fact, wildcats appear in many places, in the snow-enveloped north, in deserts and mountains and in every case have managed to evolve to fit their environments. These adaptations have filtered through to our domestic breeds: for example, the Russian Blue is an inhabitant of the Baltic region of Europe, where the climate is predominately cold, so it fortunately came equipped with a dense, luxurious 'double coat' to keep it warm. Likewise the Angora and Persians of upland Turkey and Iran also have thick coats valuable for keeping the cold at bay during the bitter continental nights. At the other extreme, the Oriental breeds have paler, silkier and thinner coats, to reflect the heat of the tropics, and which keep them correspondingly cooler.

Feral cats live in organized groups, usually in the vicinity of human populations where they can either scavenge for food or rely on food provided for them by local people. The Colosseum in Rome has such a colony where people bring them food and their way of life has changed very little for centuries. Other groups such as Egyptian

bazaar cats have an ancient linage and are to this day highly respected by the local people.

CATS AND HUMANS
Remains of cats have been found from the pre-pottery Neolithic period of Jericho (circa 7000BC), though these may have been hunted animals or the equivalent of modern feral cats, attracted to food scraps and at best tolerated. However, tamed cats have possibly lived in association with humans far earlier than archaeological and historical records imply. Cat remains (bones, teeth) are often retrieved from prehistoric sites, but it is impossible to know whether these were companions, or prey killed for their pelts and meat. Later, instead of hunting them, humans would have deliberately encouraged the presence of cats as rat catchers.

The ancient Egyptian domestic cat, which spread to Europe in historic

12

times, was used as a retriever in hunting as well as for catching rats and mice. It was probably derived from *Felis lybica* or one of the other North African wildcats. The modern domestic cat is probably descended from this animal, perhaps with an admixture of other wildcat species, or of species domesticated at various times in other parts of the world. Once the Egyptians had given up the nomadic lifestyle and learned to till the soil, they settled into agrarian communities. Since these communities depended for their very existence upon their crops, which could only be harvested once or twice a year, a means of storing them between harvests had to be found. Early on, this consisted merely of keeping grain in baskets. This attracted mice, rats and other vermin, which attracted the local lesser cat, the African Wildcat. People started encouraging the cats to stay close by to catch the vermin by leaving out scraps. Since they had a ready source of food, no threat from the people, and an absence of enemies, cats moved in on a permanent basis. Being a naturally calm species, the African Wildcat quickly adapted to people, allowing itself first to be approached, then petted, and eventually to be held. People began to appreciate the cat's other qualities: its nocturnal habits meant it hunted round

The Turkish Angora (opposite) and the Russian Blue (left) have evolved from wildcats, and like their close relatives, have coats perfectly adapted to their native environment, the Angora from the harsh uplands of Turkey, the Russian Blue from around the Baltic sea.

Feral cats have lived side by side with human beings for thousands of years and in some cultures are still greatly respected.

the clock and, unlike the dog, it was a clean animal that buried its waste outside, away from its den.

In ancient Egypt, cats were not only established as domesticated animals, but were even cherished and worshipped as gods and religious idols. This was due to their status, in this agrarian society, as rat and mouse catchers. So cherished were they, that to kill a cat, even accidentally, was an offence punishable by death. If a house-cat died, the owners shaved off their eyebrows as a sign of mourning.

Numerous cat mummies have been found; many appear to have been sacrifices and cats would have been reared in large numbers for this purpose. Paintings would seem to suggest that cats were used in the hunting of wildfowl, although this is debatable since cats are not generally good retrievers. Later, they were depicted in paintings as symbols of fertility and/or domestic harmony.

Although Ancient Egyptians forbade the export of cats, by 1700BC the cat was being depicted in domestic scenes in the Holy Land. By 1400BC domestic cats were present in Greece. By 1000BC cats had travelled northwards across the Mediterranean aboard ships (possibly with Phoenician traders) and from there they spread along trade routes. The cat travelled eastward to China and Japan (where it protected silkworm cocoons from rats). In Japan, cats were so highly valued that they were not allowed out of the house, even when a plague of rodents threatened to devastate crops.

The Romans regarded cats as rare and exotic pets, preferring the mongoose for vermin control. By 500BC, domestic cats seem to have been familiar in southern Europe. The cat may have arrived in England with the Phoenicians who traded for tin in Cornwall, though it is most likely that it was the Romans who first brought cats with them some time before AD4. Further cats arrived with the Vikings.

During the early Middle Ages, the Norse goddess Freya was the closest thing to a cat goddess among the Europeans. She was constantly surrounded by cats and her worship contained many cat-oriented rituals. When Christians barred her worship, Freya became a demon and the cat became a manifestation of the devil. Cats became associated with witches and were even believed to be able to change form from cats to witches and back at will. Thus, being a symbol of Satan, cats were burned, killed and buried alive, walled up in brick buildings, thrown off towers and tortured as part of religious rituals to drive out the devil.

The cat's popularity subsequently grew again, both on land and sea, because of its expertise in rodent control. Cats travelled alongside man in ships, valued as protectors of ships' supplies and as lucky mascots.

There was a very long period before the cat embarked on its voyage to the New World in any numbers. Although cats were taken to Quebec in the 1500s, and at least one cat accompanied the Pilgrim Fathers to America in 1620, it was not until the 1700s that domestic cats travelled to America with colonists and began to establish themselves on this continent. The cat penetrated Australia with Europeans in 1788, though aboriginal histories indicate that cats were already present on parts of the Australian coast as shipwreck survivors. There is no indigenous species of feline in Australia.

Today's Abyssinian resembles the sacred depictions of cats in Ancient Egyptian tombs.

As breeding cats for particular traits emerged, breeders began to seek out the 'natural' types of cat that occupied geographically isolated pockets of the world for cross-breeding. These included the Siamese (right), the Manx (opposite left) and the Turkish Angora (opposite right).

THE HISTORY OF SELECTIVE BREEDING

During the 19th century, important advances began to be made in the knowledge of how diseases were able to spread. As a result, cats began to be favoured as household pets in preference to dogs, being considered to be clean animals that are fastidious about their toilet. Domesticated cats interbred and in this way, almost by chance, people started to intervene in the selection and breeding of cats. Thus, the first steps along the path of producing pedigree cats were taken.

The first major British cat show was held in London's Crystal Palace in 1871, and was organized by the writer and cat artist Harrison Weir. He wanted interested people to have the opportunity of observing the different colours, markings and breeds of cat, and included newly imported Siamese cats, a Persian and an Abyssinian. The show was a huge success, and it became an annual event. Queen Victoria, who loved cats, acquired two Blue Persians. In 1887, the National Cat Club was formed, with Harrison Weir as its president, and registration procedures were instituted. This marked the beginning of the cat fancy as it is known today. The first cat show to attract wide attention in the USA, took place at Madison Square Garden, New York, in 1895. In 1899, Weir published his book *Our Cats and All About Them*, in which he set out clear and concise standards of excellence, by which all the breeds and varieties could be judged.

The London and New York shows, and others in mainland Europe, proved an enormous success and were the main impetus for modern selective breeding. The owners of pure-bred cats began to keep careful records, and so the first written pedigrees came into being. Groups interested in the same types of cats formed further clubs and societies. In 1896, the American Cat Club became North America's first registry to verify pedigrees.

At this time, the great majority of the world feline population was made up of the ubiquitous mixed-breed household cat. Breeders now began to search geographically-isolated parts of the world for these products of natural selection for the purposes of cross-breeding. The cats they found included the Turkish Angora, Siamese, Russian Blue, Manx and Abyssinian – all cats that had developed distinctive, recognizable traits setting them apart from others of their kind. These cats had developed, without human intervention, over the course of hundreds, and in some cases thousands of years.

During the 1900s, as travel became easier, breeds quickly spread across the world as it became increasingly popular to import cats from one country into another. Breeding suffered a setback during the two world wars, and some breeds, such as the Abyssinian and Russian Blue, nearly became extinct. From the late 1950s, the cat fancy expanded as knowledge of genetics grew, and many new breeds and colour varieties within breeds were developed. Some of the new breeds, such as the Somali and the Balinese, are simply longhaired versions of older, shorthaired breeds. In some instances, genetic mutations were encouraged. In others, new breed characteristics arose through haphazard mutations, resulting in such traits as stub tails, abnormally short legs, bent or curled ears, curly hair or hairlessness. While a few mutations are crippling or deadly and others merely controversial, some are nevertheless deemed desirable, so these traits were deliberately isolated and developed over generations by cat breeders. However, human intervention is not responsible for some of the most distinctive mutations. The tailless Manx from the Isle of Man and the shortened tail of the Japanese Bobtail flourished because these cats had developed in geographic isolation.

There are some people who feel that encouraging mutations has gone too far, certainly as far as aesthetics are concerned, and there has been a recent trend away from highly exaggerated looks back towards more natural, wilder-looking cats that are more sympathetic to their ancestral roots.

COAT COLOUR

The great variety in coat colour is only possible in domestic cats because they do not rely on camouflage in order to survive. The attractive colouring of most pedigree cats would spell certain death if they were left to fend for themselves in the wild. Coat colour is determined by pigment granules that occur in the shafts of each of the cat's hairs. Today, there are many variations in a cat's coat colour, but they are all derived from

RIGHT
Human intervention has created many traits and mutations in cats, some attractive, some controversial. However, some mutations, such as the Japanese Bobtail, have flourished without human help.

FAR RIGHT
The tabby pattern is also known as agouti after the rodent of that name. The fur has bands of colour which are lighter at the base and darker at the tip, and which acts as camouflage.

standard bi-colour is defined as being one-third to one-half white. 'Bi-colour' cats have white on their bellies and legs, but with patches of colour on their heads and backs. The 'Van' pattern is predominantly white but with solid patches on the head and tail only.

One of the most striking coats is the tortoiseshell, or 'tortie' pattern, in which coloured hairs occur in large distinct patches of red and black. Only female cats can have the tortoiseshell pattern because the gene can only be found on the X (female) chromosome. However, about one out of every 3,000 tri-colour cats is a male and they are usually infertile.

Black was probably the first colour mutation to appear, followed by red and then white.

only two pigments: black and red. Black was probably the first colour mutation, followed by red and then white. A dilution of black to blue was brought about by a simple mutant gene, inherited as a recessive. The pigment granules within the hair shafts are arranged in such a way that the animal appears to be slate-grey in colour. This dilution gene also works on yellow pigmentation, changing it to cream, and on chocolate, changing it to lilac.

Cats with single-coloured hair are called self or solid. Some coats are more dense and vibrant in some colours than in others. This occurs because the cat possesses a 'dense' gene, which means that each hair strand is more densely packed with pigment, creating black, chocolate, cinnamon and red. Other cats have lighter, 'dilute' coats in blue, lilac, fawn and cream.

The dominant white gene contains no pigment to mask other colours, or combine with them to create a pattern. The white cat is genetically coloured and it passes on this colour potential to its offspring. The white gene is also associated with the deafness found in some blue-eyed, white-haired cats. The

RIGHT
The tortoiseshell or 'tortie' coat is most distinctive. Only female cats display this pattern because the gene can only be found in the X (female) chromosome.

OPPOSITE LEFT
There are four basic patterns that result from the dominant tabby gene: Mackerel (also called striped), Classic (or blotched), Ticked (or Abyssinian) and Spotted. This Egyptian Mau is a Silver Spotted Tabby.

RIGHT
This Siamese has a rich cream coat with very dark brown points, which is an attractive combination and one of the most popular of the Siamese variations. It is known as Seal Point.

Breed associations make things more complicated by giving the same genetic colour a different name in different cats. For example, genetically chocolate Oriental Shorthairs are called Havana in the UK and Chestnut in North America. Meanwhile, tortie-and-white cats are called Calicos in some North American associations, while lilac cats in the UK are often called lavenders by US breeders. Differences in nomenclature are not restricted just to colours either, with Tabby Points being described as Lynx Points in North America.

Breeding standards for cats usually require the colour of their lips, noses, and paw pads to correlate with coat colour: pink in white cats, blue in blue cats, pink to brick red in reds. However, in some cases the specification can vary according to the particular breed or association.

COAT PATTERN
When cats lived in the wild, their survival depended upon their ability to blend in with their environment. Used both for hiding and for hunting, this

The pale grey coat with dark grey/black stripes makes this Mackerel Tabby most distinctive and beautiful.

camouflage was typically a banded pattern, known as agouti, like that of a tabby cat, in the colours found in their environment.

'Underneath' every cat's coat – even those coats that appear to be solid coloured – is the original tabby pattern designed to camouflage the cat in the wild, and a permanent reminder of the cat's roots. All other coat patterns are the result of genetic mutations that are encouraged through selective breeding. These mutations would have been dangerous to the cats when they lived in the wild, as their ability to hunt without being seen would have been seriously compromised. As pet cats, however, such considerations have been deemed irrelevant.

This tabby pattern known as agouti is named after a rodent of that name, which, along with other wild animals such as squirrels and mice, shares this patterning. In agouti patterning, each hair of the fur contains bands of colour that are lighter at the base and darker towards the tip. These markings are what camouflage the cat in its environment. In domestic cats, they are often more apparent on kittens and gradually fade with maturity. Although the agouti gene is dominant, solid colours can exist in selectively bred cats because of the recessive non-agouti gene.

There are four basic patterns that result from the dominant tabby gene: Mackerel (also called striped), Classic (or blotched), Ticked (or Abyssinian) and Spotted. Mackerel stripes are narrow, parallel and run from the spine down the flanks to the belly. This pattern was predominant in Europe until a few hundred years ago, when it was superseded by the classic tabby pattern. Classic tabbies have wide stripes that form swirls on the flanks. The markings on ticked tabbies are restricted to the head, legs and tail and the body is softly flecked.

Shading is the result of the 'I', or inhibitor, gene. The I gene permits only the ends of the cat hair to retain pigment, resulting in subtle coat patterns that appear to change as the cat moves. In self cats, it creates a 'smoke' pattern, with a white undercoat. In agouti coats, the colour is more restricted. Different degrees of shading create 'shaded', 'silver' and 'silver tabby' coats, and 'tipped' coats, which are only barely coloured – known as 'frosting'. Another distinctive coat pattern is referred to as 'pointing', most commonly seen in Siamese cats. The coat is light with dark areas, or 'points', on the muzzle, ears, feet and tail. In male cats, the hair is also darker on the scrotum.

Physical features, such as folded ears, are more indicative of breed than the colour or pattern of the coat. This is a Scottish Fold Cat.

Interestingly, this colouring is temperature-sensitive: if skin temperature is lower, a special enzyme is activated that darkens the coat colour. It is also affected by age, with Siamese kittens being pale at birth and then they often develop shading on their bodies in middle age, particularly in the case of darker varieties such as Seal Points.

BODY FORM

A cat's facial features, body shape and other physical characteristics, such as folded ears, are more indicative of breed than the colour or pattern of the coat, which are often similar across the different breeds. As these physical characteristics developed, as the breed adapted to its environment; they can also be indicators of a breed's personality. For

RIGHT

Cats originating from colder climates tend to have stocky, solid bodies, rounded heads, and shortish noses. They also have long, thick coats. This Maine Coon is a good example.

example, leaner breeds tend to be more lively than more compact breeds.

Certain physical characteristics can also be attributed to the cat's place of origin. Cats that have originated in colder climates – especially Northern Europe – have stocky, solid and sturdy bodies, large, rounded heads, moderately short, broad muzzles and short, thick tails. To endure the cold environment, their bodies are structured to retain body heat. The Maine Coon and the Norwegian Forest Cat are good examples of this category.

Semi-foreign breeds that originated in the warmer climates of Africa and Asia are more slender and muscular than their cold-weather counterparts, and are quite elegant, with moderately wedge-shaped heads, oval paws and long, gently tapering tails. On their slender but muscular legs, they stand taller than those cats from colder climates. Semi-foreign breeds are currently popular with cat breeders, and many of the recently recognized breeds in the world fall into this category. Examples of these cats are the Abyssinian and Turkish Angora. Some of the more recent efforts to create wild-looking cats, such as the Ocicat, use semi-foreign parent breeds and this is reflected in their type.

Oriental breeds, which originated in hot, tropical countries, are the most

dramatically slender cats, with long bodies and long, thin tails. To keep the cats cool in the warm climate, their bodies are designed to let heat escape by having the maximum surface area for their size. The Siamese, with its wedge-shaped head and large ears, is a perfect example of this breed. Newer breeds have been created that mimic the Oriental style. The Oriental Shorthair, for example, is the solid-coloured version of the Siamese. Other Western breeds, such as the Cornish and Devon Rexes, have been bred to look rather like Oriental breeds.

EYE SHAPE AND COLOUR

Like cats themselves, cats' eyes are exotic and beautiful. These windows of mystery range in colour from the golden copper and yellow of the wildcat, to the yellow, green and blue found in domestic breeds. Most eye colours are not governed by coat colour. The only exception is white-coated cats with blue eyes. Blue is the eye colour of all new-born kittens. Blue eyes lack pigment, allowing more light to enter the eye. This lack of pigmentation affects the colour of the coat, too, and occurs in cats with a high degree of white in their coats. Unfortunately, white cats with blue eyes are often deaf because the gene that results in their lack of

pigmentation also causes the fluid to dry up in the inner ear soon after birth, preventing the effective transmission of sound waves through to the auditory nerve. Sadly, there is no treatment for this condition. The blue eyes of Siamese cats are not linked to deafness, but may be associated, instead, with poor three-dimensional vision.

The cat's breed may also be indicated by the shape of its eyes. Although most wildcats typically have slanted oval eyes, the eye shapes of domestic cats have been altered through centuries of cross-breeding. Round, prominent eyes can be indicative of the original Western breeds as well as some Eastern, while slanted, almond-shaped eyes are common to Oriental and foreign breeds.

LEFT
Cats' eyes are beautiful and mysterious, and range through yellow, copper and green to the deepest blue. Most are oval in shape, but through selective breeding, those of Western breeds have become more rounded, while the eyes of Orientals are slanted.

Many people would always choose a non-pedigree cat (right), as they are particularly robust and usually live to a ripe old age. They are also resistant to many diseases; but above all, they can be sure that each one is unique. Pedigree cats, on the other hand, are valued for the particular characteristics of their breed; for example, the Siamese for its sleek appearance and out-going personality, or the Burmese (opposite) for its beautiful coat and striking eyes. If this is the case, always buy from a reputable breeder.

CHOOSING A CAT

There are many different types of cat from which to choose and they come in a variety of shapes and colours. The first choice is between pedigree and non-pedigree. Some people are attracted to pedigree cats because they admire certain characteristics which have become recognizable in a particular breed. For example, a Siamese may be preferred for its exotic appearance and flamboyant nature, or one might yearn for a Persian with its beautiful luxuriant coat. Unless you know of a particular kitten or cat at a rescue centre, the best way of obtaining a pedigree cat is directly from a breeder. In this way you will be certain of the cat's origins, who has been caring for it, its medical history and its parentage. Reputable breeders always ensure their cats are given a thorough health check by a vet, as well as the required inoculations for their ages before releasing then to new homes. Pedigree cats do not come cheap, so be prepared for a high price tag. Make sure you read up on the breed of your choice as some are more prone to certain diseases than others. Take into account the amount of attention it may require; longhaired breeds need a thorough daily grooming session.

Pedigree cats tend to look more striking and exotic than their mixed-bred

cousins, so bear in mind that the possibility of theft is correspondingly greater. For this reason, you may decide to construct a run in your garden to restrict your cat from roaming.

Should you decide that a non-pedigree or 'moggie' is for you, you may have made a wise decision. They are robust, hardy, more resistant to disease than pedigree cats and are readily available from rescue centres. An attractive feature of non-pedigree cats is that although they are all beautiful, each one is unique and has its own particular characteristics.

INTRODUCTION TO BREEDS

RIGHT

*Because the selective
breeding of cats has
happened comparatively
recently, many breeds are
not far removed from
their original type. This
Turkish Angora has
changed little from its
cousins which once
roamed the central
uplands around Ankara.*

BELOW RIGHT

*The modern Sphynx
breeding programme
began in 1966 in Toronto,
Canada, when an
ordinary shorthaired
black-and-white
domestic cat gave birth
to a hairless male kitten.
The breed was developed
from this mother and
son, and subsequently,
crosses with Devon Rexes
were used to expand the
breed's bloodline.*

It is only comparatively recently in the history of cats that they have been domesticated, and selective breeding is still in its relative infancy. As a result, the range of cat breeds is quite small when compared with dogs, and domestic cats still – with a few exceptions, such as the Sphynx – very much resemble their wild ancestors. There is also much less diversity between the different breeds compared with dogs. One of the main reasons, for example, that different cat breeds are broadly of similar size, is the fact that the African Wildcat – ancestor of today's domestic cat breeds – does not vary significantly in size throughout its range. On the other hand, the Grey Wolf – which is the original ancestor of the domestic dog – varies hugely in size across its range and, therefore, domestic dogs vary greatly in size, too.

HYBRIDIZATION

Thanks to advances in DNA technology, studies of the domestic cat's genetic history are now a reality, and so it may become possible in the future to confirm the origins of breeds, as well as their relationships to each other. What is already evident is that, until very recently, there was no other input into their genetic development than from the African Wildcat. It is now considered possible that the longhaired gene was introduced as a result of natural hybridization between domestic cats roaming free and Pallas' Cat, a species found in Asia. Although interest in wildcat crossings has been sparked in recent years by the huge rise in popularity of the Bengal breed, hybridization between wild species of cat and their domestic relatives is nothing new. As long ago as the late 1800s, cat shows had classes for the offspring of such matings. However,

none of these hybrids was subsequently developed into a breed at that stage.

In the USA, a number of breeds are currently being developed from wild cats, but recent restrictions on the keeping of such animals as pets looked as though they might put paid to this trend and that there would therefore be little scope for developing new breeds by further hybridization. However, the development of new breeds continues apace. It remains to be seen, though, whether any will attain the popularity of the Bengal.

LEFT
During the 1970s, an American cat breeder found a colony of unusual-looking feral cats in Singapore. Some of these were taken to the USA in 1975 and today all registered Singapuras come from this original breeding programme.

LONGHAIR GROUP

RIGHT

There is some confusion surrounding the use of the name Javanese in the cat world, although it is always used to describe cats of distinctly Oriental type.

OPPOSITE

The luxuriantly-coated Persian cat has a gentle disposition and is happy to live indoors. Its long coat requires daily grooming to maintain its beauty and keep it free from knots.

The true longhaired cat is the Persian, also sometimes known as the Longhair. The breed is probably descended from matings between Angora cats, which originated from the Ankara region of Turkey, with others from Persia (now Iran). It is said that the first examples of these longhaired cats reached Italy and France in the 16th century. It wasn't until the middle of the 19th century that the cats acquired pedigree status. Persians are now bred in a staggering array of colours and patterns.

The typical Persian cat has a luxuriously silky coat that consists of long guard hairs and shorter down hairs. Unfortunately, because of the nature of their coats, even the most fastidious self-grooming Longhair will still need daily grooming by its owner. If you are considering owning a Longhair, the time taken for such regular grooming must be taken into consideration, as well as the fact that being year-round moulters, your carpets, clothes and furniture are likely to be liberally coated with cat's hairs, too. However, there is no denying the unbeatable opulence – and placid, friendly nature – of the Persian cat.

PERSIAN

Origins The ancestors of the Persian Longhair (known as Persian in the USA) were stocky, longhaired grey cats imported from Persia (now Iran) into Italy in the 17th century, and silken-haired white Angora cats from Turkey that arrived in France at about the same time. In the late 1800s, the Persian was developed in the UK with the black being the first to be accorded a formal breeding standard. The original stocky build is still an essential mark of today's Longhair breed, although other characteristics have been dramatically altered. By the beginning of the 1900s, the breed had been recognized by all registries.

Appearance The body is massive and powerful, with a short neck, a broad chest, and short, stocky legs. The paws are large and round, and may be tufted. The head is big and round, with small, round-tipped ears and a short, broad nose. The eyes are large, round and set wide apart. The tail is short but very full to match the luxurious coat.

Coat The Longhair has a full and flowing coat of long, dense fur that tangles easily and needs daily brushing and combing to prevent matting. The fur around the neck is extra long, forming the typical ruff.

Characteristics and Temperament
Quiet and affectionate, but somewhat detached, the Longhair is ideally suited to living in an apartment, as it prefers to be indoors, but may also enjoy outdoor life. It is the breed most likely to accept other cats into its home. These cats are gentle by nature, and as kittens are playful and mischievous.

WHITE

Origins The result of matings between the earliest imported Angora and Persian cats. The original, blue-eyed variety was prone to deafness, so it was cross-bred with Blue and Black Persians. Some of these offspring had blue eyes, but some had copper-coloured eyes, and others had one orange or copper eye and one blue eye. These odd-eyed Whites are likely to be deaf on the blue-eyed side of the face. Today's White Persians are judged as three separate varieties, according to eye colour, in the UK.

Grooming Daily care is needed, as all white varieties can become soiled with yellow staining around the eyes, nostrils, lips and under the tail. White grooming powder is available which both cleans and guards against staining.

Colouring A pure, glistening white coat, without markings or shadings.

Nose leather and paw pads are pink. In the blue-eyed White, eye colour is deep blue. In the copper-eyed (USA) or orange-eyed (UK) White, eye colour is a brilliant copper (USA) or copper or orange (UK). The odd-eyed White has one eye of deep blue, the other of orange or copper.

BLACK

Origins The earliest Persian breed to have been officially recognized; today, however, it is quite rare.

Coat The glossy, raven-black coat is prone to developing rusty tinges, thought to be caused by strong sunlight or damp conditions. To maintain the coat, therefore, the cat needs to be kept in cool, dry conditions free from direct light. Periods of moulting may also cause brownish bars to appear on the coat.

Colouring Dense coal-black coat from roots to tips of the hair and free from any tinge, markings or shadings. Nose leather is black. Paw pads are black or brown. Eye colour is brilliant copper (USA) or copper or deep orange (UK).

RED

Origins Until quite recently, the Red Persian was one of the rarest of all feline varieties. This was largely because of the need to select parents that had displayed

A Red Persian kitten. These are quite rare as they should be pure red with no tabby markings. This little chap is not quite perfect as he has some tabby in his coat, but he is very appealing nonetheless.

few if any tabby markings as kittens, combined with long fur and intensity of colour.

Colouring Deep, rich, clear, brilliant red coat without markings, shadings or ticking. Lips and chin are the same colour as the coat. Nose leather and paw pads are brick red and eye colour is brilliant copper (USA) or deep copper (UK).

CREAM

Origins The Cream Persian is a dilute Red, with probable input from the white Angoras that were cross-bred with Persians in the 1880s. At first, cream cats were often discarded by exhibitors in favour of cats with stronger coat colours. In the early 20th century, Creams were eventually imported into the USA from the UK and soon established themselves as successful show winners. Faint tabby markings usually disappear as kittens mature.

Colouring Requirements differ between the USA, the UK and Europe. The CFA (Cat Fanciers' Association) requires one level shade of buff cream, sound to the roots, without markings. The UK's GCCF (Governing Council of the Cat Fancy) requires a pure pale to medium colour, without shadings or markings. The FIFe (Fédération Internationale Féline) standard requires pale, pure pastel cream with no warm tone or any lighter shadings or markings. Nose leather and paw pads are pink. Eye colour is brilliant copper (USA) and deep copper (UK).

BLUE

A **b**lue coat should be even in tone and free from all markings, shadings or white hairs. Nose leather and paw pads are blue. Eye colour is brilliant copper (USA), copper or deep orange (UK).

BLUE-CREAM

Origins Blue-Creams were at first only produced by accident in the days before the genetics of coat colour were understood, and was not recognized until 1930. The colour is in fact, the dilute equivalent of tortoiseshell, so the Blue-Cream Persian has patches of blue and cream, just as a tortoiseshell has patches of black and red,.

Colouring In the USA, the coat is blue with clearly defined patches of solid cream, well broken on both body and extremities. The UK's GCCF requires a coat of mingled pastel shades of blue and cream. In Europe, FIFe refers to the Blue-Cream as the Blue Tortie and requires a light blue-grey and pale cream coat, patched and /or mingled,

both colours to be evenly distributed over the body and extremities. Eye colour is brilliant copper (USA), deep copper or orange (UK).

LILAC-CREAM

Colouring In general, requirements for coat colour and pattern differ between the USA, the UK and Europe. In the USA, the coat is lilac with clearly defined patches of solid cream, well broken on both body and extremities. The UK's GCCF requires a coat of pastel shades of lilac and cream, softly intermingled. In Europe, FIFe refers to Lilac-Cream as Lilac Tortie and requires a light lilac and pale cream coat, patched and/or mingled, both colours to be evenly distributed over the body and extremities. Eye colour is brilliant copper (USA) or deep copper or orange (UK).

CHOCOLATE

Origins The Chocolate Persian derives from the mating of a Chocolate Point Siamese with a Blue Persian. Through generations of breeding, however, the Chocolate has established itself as a variety in its own right.

Colouring The coat is a rich, warm chocolate brown, sound from roots to tip of fur with no shading, markings or white hairs. The nose leather is brown

and the paw pads are pink. Eye colour is brilliant copper.

LILAC

Origins Another offshoot from the breeding programme for Colourpoint Longhairs was the Lilac Persian. These cats have some Siamese in them, which may account for their independent, yet affectionate, natures.

Colouring The coat is a rich, warm lavender with a pinkish tone, sound from roots to tip of fur with no shading, markings or white hairs. The nose leather is lavender and the paw pads are pink. Eye colour is brilliant copper.

BI-COLOUR

Origin At first, longhaired cats with patches of white were disqualified from shows, but eventually, these 'magpies' or bi-colours were allowed to compete and eventually new standards were drawn up by cat associations globally.

Colouring Black, blue, red or cream, all with white on feet, legs, underside, chest and muzzle. Newer variants are chocolate and lilac bi-colour variants. Not more than two-thirds of the coat to be coloured and not more than half of the coat to be white. Eyes brilliant copper (USA). Not more than two-thirds

A Chocolate Persian. This colour was achieved by mating a Chocolate Point Siamese with a Blue Persian to create part of the formula for the Persian Colourpoint.

of the coat to be coloured and not more than half of the coat to be white. Eyes brilliant copper or deep orange. (UK)

PERSIAN VAN BI-COLOUR

Colouring Any solid colour with white. Colour distribution is different from that of the Bi-colour, being a white cat with the colour confined to head, legs and tail.

PEWTER

Origins A relatively recent development is the breeding from Tortie Cameos which produces kittens with black rather than red, cream or tortoiseshell tipping.

Colouring Very similar in appearance to Shaded Silvers, but with orange or copper eye colour.

SMOKE

Origins Black Smokes were the first of this colour to be bred. At first they were considered to be rather poorer versions of the Blue Persian, and as such were kept as domestic companions rather than as show cats. At a UK cat show in 1893, the Smoke Persian was given its own breed class and enjoyed a certain popularity for a time at the beginning of the 20th century. However, since then the breed has declined and is nowadays a rarity. In the USA, however, the story has been different, where it has always found favour and has begun, more recently, to be bred in other colours than black.

Black Smoke Undercoat is pure white, deeply tipped with black. Mask and points are black. The frill and ear tufts are light silver. Nose leather and paw pads are black. Eye colour is brilliant copper (USA) or orange or copper (UK).

Blue Smoke Undercoat is pure white, deeply tipped with blue. Mask and points are blue. The frill and ear tufts are light silver. Nose leather and paw pads are blue. Eye colour is brilliant copper or orange or copper.

Red Smoke Undercoat is pure white, deeply tipped with red. Mask and points are red. The frill and ear tufts are white. Nose leather and paw pads are rose. Eye colour is brilliant copper.

Lilac Smoke Undercoat is pure white, deeply tipped with lilac. Mask and points are lilac. The frill and ear tufts are white. Nose leather and paw pads are lavender-pink. Eye colour is brilliant copper or orange.

Chocolate Smoke Undercoat is pure white, deeply tipped with chocolate.

Mask and points are chocolate. The frill and ear tufts are white. Nose leather and paw pads are brown with a rosy tone. Eye colour is brilliant copper or orange.

Tortoiseshell Smoke Undercoat is pure white, deeply tipped with black, with clearly defined unbrindled patches of red and light red hairs in the pattern of a Tortoiseshell. The frill and ear tufts are white. Eye colour is brilliant copper.

Blue-Cream Smoke Undercoat is pure white, deeply tipped with blue and cream with clearly defined unbrindled patches of cream hairs in the pattern of a Blue-Cream. The frill and ear tufts are white. Eye colour is brilliant copper or orange.

Chocolate Tortoiseshell Smoke Undercoat is pure white, deeply tipped with chocolate and light red. Mask and points are chocolate-tortoiseshell. The frill and ear tufts are white. Nose leather and paw pads are mottled. Eye colour is brilliant copper or orange.

Lilac-Cream Smoke Undercoat is pure white, deeply tipped with lilac and cream. Mask and points are lilac-cream. The frill and ear tufts are white. Nose leather and paw pads are mottled. Eye colour is brilliant copper or orange.

CAMEO

Origins This colour was first bred in the USA during the 1950s. There are three varieties of shading in cameos, which take a while to develop. These are Shell, Shaded and Smoke. Due to their exceptionally friendly nature and their particularly unusual coat-colouring, these cats have become immensely popular worldwide.

Cream Shell Cameo The white undercoat is tipped with faint cream on the head, back, flanks and tail to give a sparkling appearance. Face and legs may be slightly tipped. Chin, ear tufts, stomach and chest are distinctly whitish. Eye rims, nose leather and paw pads are pink. Eye colour is brilliant copper.

Cream Shaded Cameo The white undercoat is tipped with a more definite cream coloration, especially on the mantle. Chin, stomach and chest are paler. Eye rims, nose leather and paw pads are pink. Eye colour is brilliant copper.

Red Shell Cameo The white undercoat is tipped with slight red tipping. The sides of the body are paler than the area along the spine. Eye rims, nose leather and paw pads are rose. Eye colour is brilliant copper.

Red Shaded Cameo The white undercoat has an even red shading, creating a red mantle, but is less intense again on the frill, flanks and underside of the body. Eye colour is brilliant copper.

TABBY

Silver Tabby The ground colour of pure pale silver includes the lips and chin. Markings are dense black. Nose leather is brick red. Paw pads are black and eye colour is green or hazel.

Red Tabby The ground colour of red includes the lips and chin. Markings are a deep, rich red. Nose leather is brick red. Paw pads are deep pink and eye colour is brilliant copper.

Brown Tabby The ground colour of the cot is a brilliant coppery-brown. Markings are dense black. Nose leather is brick red. Paw pads are black or brown and eye colour is copper or hazel.

Blue Tabby The ground colour of pale bluish-fawn includes the lips and chin. Markings are very deep blue. Nose leather is old rose or blue. Paw pads are dark blue and eye colour is copper or orange.

Cream Tabby The ground colour of very pale cream includes the lips and chin.

Markings are buff or cream. Nose leather and paw pads are pink and eye colour is brilliant copper.

Cameo Tabby The off-white ground colour includes lips and chin. Markings are red. Nose leather and paw pads are rose and eye colour is brilliant copper.

Silver Tortie Tabby The ground colour of pale silver includes the lips and chin, with classic or mackerel markings of black and patches of red and/or light red on the body and extremities. Eye colour is brilliant copper or hazel.

Brown Tortie Tabby A ground colour of brilliant coppery-brown, with lips and chin the same colour as the rings around the eyes. There are classic or mackerel markings of black and patches of red and/or light red on body and extremities. Eye colour is brilliant copper.

Blue Tortie Tabby The ground colour of pale bluish-ivory includes the lips and chin. There are classic or mackerel markings of very deep blue and patches of cream on the body and extremities. Eye colour is brilliant copper.

TORTOISESHELL

Origins It was not until the beginning of the 20th century that tortoiseshell

Persians first made an appearance at cat shows. They have become extremely popular, not only because their docile nature makes them ideal as pets, but also because of the intriguing fact that all variations of tortoiseshell are usually female. This occurs because of the complexity of their genetic inheritance.

Colouring The coat is clearly patched in black with light and dark red. Nose leather and paw pads are pink or black. Eyes are brilliant copper or deep orange.

TORTOISESHELL-AND-WHITE

Origins This version of Tortoiseshell was once named Chintz in the UK, but the name is no longer used. In the USA, this variety is called Calico, after the cotton cloth of that name.

Colouring A white coat with clear patches of black, light red and dark red. Nose leather and paw pads are pink or black. Eyes are brilliant copper or deep orange.

CALICO (USA)

Colouring Body colour is white with unbrindled patches of black and red. White is predominant on the underparts. Eye colour is brilliant copper.

DILUTE CALICO

Colouring Body colour is white with

unbrindled patches of blue and cream. White is predominant on the underparts. Eye colour is brilliant copper.

CHOCOLATE TORTOISESHELL

Colouring The coat is clearly patched with chocolate and light red. Nose leather and paw pads are pink or black. Eyes are brilliant copper or deep orange.

CHINCHILLA

Origins The Chinchilla dates back to the late 19th century in the UK, and occurred as the result of an accidental mating between a female silver tabby and a male cat of another colour. By the beginning of the 20th century these cats were being imported from the UK into the USA and have continued to gain popularity in both countries.

Colouring Pure white undercoat, sufficiently tipped with black to give a sparkling effect. Eyes and lips outlined with black. Nose leather is brick red. Paw pads are black. Eyes are emerald or aquamarine.

CHINCHILLA GOLDEN

Colouring Rich cream undercoat tipped with seal brown to give a golden effect. Eyes and lips outlined with seal brown. Nose leather is deep rose. Paw pads are seal brown. Eyes are emerald or aquamarine.

OPPOSITE
A Silver Tabby Persian.

RIGHT and OPPOSITE
The Shaded Golden Persian has a warm, rich coat with a cream undercoat and a mantle of seal tipping.

SHADED SILVER

Colouring Pure white undercoat with a mantle of black shading. Eyes and lips are outlined in black. Nose leather is brick red. Paw pads are black or seal. Eyes are emerald or aquamarine.

SHADED GOLDEN

Colouring Rich, warm cream undercoat with a mantle of seal brown tipping, shading down the face, sides and tail. Eyes and lips are outlined in seal brown. Nose leather is deep rose. Paw pads are seal brown. Eyes are emerald or aquamarine.

COLOURPOINT LONGHAIR

(Himalayan)

Origins Experiments in crossing a Longhair and a Siamese began in the early 20th century. The result was the Colourpoint Longhair – cats of the typical longhair, Persian type but with deeper colour restricted to the cat's 'points'. These are the extremities: the face (or mask), the ears, legs, paws and tail. The breed had been accepted in the UK and the USA during the 1950s and by the 1960s, the breed was recognized worldwide.

Appearance The Colourpoint is of medium to large build and stocky. The head is round and massive and the eyes large, full and round. The ears are small and round-tipped. The paws are large, round and firm and the tail is short but in proportion.

Coat The coat is thick, dense and glossy with no trace of woolliness. There is a full frill over the shoulders, continuing between the front legs. Thorough daily grooming is required to keep the coat in good condition, paying particular attention to the underparts between the hind and fore legs, under the tail, and around the neck.

Characteristics and Temperament As one might expect, the Colourpoint has inherited some of the best traits of its ancestry. These cats tend to be more lively than the typical placid Persian but not as noisy as a Siamese. They are calm and friendly and make relaxed but outgoing companions.

Solid Point:

Seal Point Pale fawn or cream body, which shades gradually into a lighter colour on the chest and belly. Points are deep seal brown. Nose leather and paw pads are the same colour as the points. Eye colour is deep, vivid blue.

Blue Point Bluish-white body, which shades gradually into white on the chest and belly. Points are blue. Nose leather and paw pads are slate grey. Eye colour is deep, vivid blue.

Chocolate Point Ivory body, with no shading. Points are milk chocolate. Nose leather and paw pads are cinnamon pink. Eye colour is deep, vivid blue.

Lilac Point Glacial white body, with no shading. Points are frosty grey with a pinkish tone. Nose leather and paw pads are lavender-pink. Eye colour is deep, vivid blue.

Red Point Creamy-white body. Points are deep orange flame to deep red. Nose leather and paw pads are flesh pink or coral pink. Eye colour is deep, vivid blue.

Cream Point Creamy-white body with no shading. Points are buff cream. Nose leather and paw pads are flesh pink or salmon coral. Eye colour is deep, vivid blue.

Tortie Point Creamy-white or pale fawn body. Points are seal brown with unbrindled patches of red or light red. Nose leather and paw pads are seal brown with flesh and/or coral pink mottling. Eye colour is deep, vivid blue.

Blue-Cream Point Bluish-white or creamy-white body, which shades gradually to white on the chest and belly. Points are blue with patches of cream. Nose leather and paw pads are slate grey or pink, or slate grey and pink mottling. Eye colour is deep, vivid blue.

Tabby Point:

Seal Tabby Point Pale cream to fawn body. Mask is clearly lined with dark stripes: vertical lines on the forehead form the classic 'M' shape. Inner ear is light and there is a 'thumbprint' on the back of the outer ear. Points are beige-brown ticked with darker brown tabby markings. Nose leather is seal or brick red. Paw pads are seal brown. Eyes are deep, vivid blue.

Blue Tabby Point Bluish-white body. Mask is clearly lined with dark stripes: vertical lines on the forehead form the classic M shape. Inner ear is light and there is a thumbprint on the back of the outer ear. Points are light silvery-blue ticked with darker blue tabby markings. Nose leather is blue or brick red. Paw

pads are blue. Eyes are deep, vivid blue.

Chocolate Tabby Point Ivory body. Mask is clearly lined with dark stripes: vertical lines on the forehead form the classic M shape. Inner ear is light and there is a thumbprint on the back of the outer ear. Points are warm fawn ticked with milk chocolate markings. Nose leather and paw pads are cinnamon pink. Eyes are deep, vivid blue.

Lilac Tabby Point Glacial white body.

Mask is clearly lined with dark stripes: vertical lines on the forehead form the classic M shape. Inner ear is light and there is a thumbprint on the back of the outer ear. Points are frosty-grey ticked with darker frosty tabby markings. Nose leather and paw pads are lavender-pink. Eyes are deep, vivid blue.

CHOCOLATE AND LILAC
Chocolate Longhair Rich, warm chocolate-brown coat, sound from roots

to tips of hair and free from markings, shadings or white hairs. Nose leather and paw pads are brown. Eye colour is brilliant copper (USA) or deep orange or copper (UK).

Lilac Longhair Rich, warm lavender coat, sound from roots to tips of hair and free from markings, shadings or white hairs. Nose leather and paw pads are pink. Eye colour is brilliant copper (USA) or pale orange (UK).

The Colourpoint Longhair is the result of crossing a Siamese with a Persian. This example is a Red Point.

Like all Orientals, the Javanese has an outgoing personality and is quite demanding of attention. They crave human company and won't tolerate being left alone for very long.

JAVANESE

Origins There is a lot of confusion surrounding the use of this name in the cat world, although it is always used to describe cats of distinctly Oriental type. It has been adopted simply because of the tradition which has grown up for using the names of countries and islands from south-eastern Asia for other Oriental breeds, such as the Siamese and Balinese. Unfortunately, it has been used to describe different cats in the past, rather than being applied to a particular breed. The longhaired form of the Oriental is now perhaps best-known under this description, having been bred from crosses between Orientals and longhairs of Oriental type.

But some US cat organizations adopted this description for the non-traditional varieties of the Balinese, notably the red, tortie and tabby varieties of this pointed breed rather than solid-coloured Longhaired Orientals. As a result, the description of Javanese may be applied both to solid and colourpointed cats, depending on the show classification. In the UK, this description was also used for a period for cats which were evolved in the breeding programme which gave rise to the Angora, the modern re-creation of the ancient Turkish Angora breed, adding still further to the confusion over the use of this breed name.

44

Javanese were bred from Oriental and long-coated cats of Oriental type. They have long tapering legs and a svelte body and are strikingly beautiful. The varieties of coat colour are similar to other Oriental breeds. Below are two Lilac Point kittens, with a Red Point adult cat opposite.

Appearance The Javanese, as a Longhaired Oriental, has a wedge-shaped head and medium-sized, almond-shaped eyes. The ears are large and pointed and the body is long, svelte, well muscled but dainty, with the shoulders no wider than the hips. The cat has long, fine legs ending in small, dainty, oval paws. The tail is very long and thin and tapers to a point, with the hair spread out like a plume.

Coat The coat is fine and silky, medium-long on the body and without an undercoat. There is a frill round the shoulders and chest. Regular gentle brushing keeps the coat in good condition.

Characteristics and Temperament
Active, always alert and very inquisitive, the Javanese has an extrovert personality and is intelligent and quite vocal. It is a very affectionate cat and loves human company. It hates to be left alone for long periods.

Javanese Varieties
Typical colours are as for the Oriental Shorthair – black, blue, chocolate, lilac, red, cream, cinnamon, fawn, tortoiseshell (all colours), smoke (all colours), tabby (all colours), tabby-tortoiseshell or torbie (all colours). The eye colour for all colour varieties is a vivid, intense green or blue.

Semi-Longhair Group

Some breeds of longhaired cats are more accurately referred to as semi-longhairs. The distinctive feature that sets semi-longhairs apart from true longhairs is the length of their underfur. This is significantly shorter than that of their guard hairs, whereas in Longhairs, they are of similar length. As a result, the longer fur of the semi-longhair lies flatter, particularly when the coat becomes thinner in the warmer months of the year, accounting for their resemblance to shorthaired cats at this stage. Coat care is more easily achieved

in semi-longhairs, compared to genuine Longhairs because it is less dense, lies flatter and is less easily matted. Regular grooming is required, but at nothing like the level of that required of a true Longhair. Semi-longhairs, therefore, are a good choice of cat for the pet owner who enjoys the look of the Longhair, but not the hard work of constant brushing. Many semi-longhair breeds, such as the Maine Coone, owe their long fur to their ancestral habitat and the necessity to develop protective 'clothing' in harsh environments. However, others, such as the Cymric, are newer breeds, developed purely because of the aesthetic pleasure of their luxurious coats.

OPPOSITE LEFT
Maine Coons are large, sweet-natured animals, considered by many to be the ideal pet cat. They are slow to mature and may take up to four years to attain full adult stature.

RIGHT
Birmans are proud, intelligent and inquisitive. They love people and are extremely loyal.

LEFT
Ragdolls are placid and don't mind being handled. They are likely to appeal to bird-lovers as they have little interest in hunting.

The Balinese is similar to the Siamese in appearance and temperament. In fact, it is sometimes referred to as the Longhair Siamese.

BALINESE

Origins Once known as the Longhair Siamese, the Balinese is a silky, longer-haired version of the Siamese cat. The cat's gracefulness and lithe build are reminiscent of the temple dancers of the Indonesian island of Bali, in whose honour the breed is named. The long-coated kittens that sometimes appear in litters of Siamese cats were developed into the Balinese in the USA in the 1950s. The new breed was introduced to the UK and Europe in the 1970s.

Appearance The Balinese is of medium build, but long-limbed and lithe. It has a long, wedge-shaped head, wide between the ears and narrowing to the nose, which is long and straight. The cat's most distinctive feature is its almond-shaped, slanted sapphire blue eyes. The ears are large and pointed, and the tail is very long and thin, with hair spread out like a plume.

Coat Since it has no undercoat, the Balinese's long and typically pale-coloured fine top coat feels exceptionally silky and lies flat to the body. The colourpoint fur can be in a range of colours and patterns. The coat needs regular gentle combing, while the tail should be brushed.

Characteristics and Temperament Not surprisingly, Balinese are similar in temperament to the Siamese. They love to be the centre of attention and want to be part of the family, amusing people with their acrobatic antics. They are usually affectionate but can be aloof. Although they are a little quieter than their Siamese cousins, their voices are penetrating nonetheless.

Balinese Varieties
In the UK, all colour varieties are called Balinese, but in the USA it is only the

four traditional colours – Seal Point, Blue Point, Chocolate Point and Lilac Point that are recognized as such. Others are more usually known as Javanese (see page 44).

Solid Point:

Seal Point Pale fawn to cream body. Dark seal brown points, nose leather and paw pads.

Blue Point Glacial white body with no cream tinge. Blue-grey points, nose leather and paw pads.

Chocolate Point Ivory body. Points are milk chocolate. Chocolate nose leather and paw pads.

Lilac Point Off-white body. Points are pinkish-grey. Pinkish/faded-grey nose leather and paw pads.

Red Point White shading to apricot body. Points are bright reddish-gold. Pink nose leather and paw pads.

Cream Point Creamy-white body. Points are pastel cream. Pink nose leather and paw pads.

Apricot Point Warm creamy-white body. Points are hot cream. Pink nose leather and paw pads.

Tortie Point:

Seal Tortie Point Cream shading to fawn body. Points are seal brown patched with red. Seal brown and/or pink nose leather and paw pads.

Blue Tortie Point Glacial white body. Points are light blue with shades of cream. Light blue or pink nose leather and paw pads.

Chocolate Tortie Point Ivory body. Points are milk chocolate with shades of red. Milk chocolate or pink nose leather and paw pads.

Lilac Tortie Point Off-white body. Points are pinkish-grey with shades of cool-toned cream. Pale pink or lavender-pink nose leather and paw pads.

Cinnamon Tortie Point Ivory body. Points are warm cinnamon brown with shades of red. Cinnamon brown or pink nose leather and paw pads.

Caramel Tortie Point Off-white body. Points are brownish-grey with shades of apricot. Brownish-grey or pink nose leather and paw pads.

Fawn Tortie Point Off-white body. Points are pale rosy mushroom with shades of cream. Mushroom or pink nose leather and paw pads.

Tabby Point:

Seal Tabbie Point Beige body. Points are dark seal tabby. Eye and nose rims are seal brown. Brick red, pink or seal brown nose leather. Paw pads are seal brown.

Blue Tabby Point Bluish-white body. Points are blue-grey tabby. Eye and nose rims are blue-grey. Old rose or blue-grey nose leather. Paw pads are blue-grey.

Chocolate Tabby Point Ivory body. Points are milk chocolate tabby. Eye and nose rims are milk chocolate. Light red, pink or milk chocolate nose leather. Paw pads are cinnamon to milk chocolate.

Lilac Tabby Point Glacial white body. Points are lilac tabby. Eye and nose rims are lavender-pink. Lavender-pink or pink nose leather. Paw pads are lavender-pink.

Red Tabby Point Off-white body with slight red tinge. Points are warm orange tabby. Eye and nose rims are dark pink. Brick red or pink nose leather. Paw pads are pink.

Cream Tabby Point Creamy-white body. Points are cream tabby. Eye and nose rims are dark pink. Pink nose leather and paw pads.

Seal Tortie Tabby Point Beige body. Points colour has seal tabby markings mingled with red tortie markings. Nose rims are seal. Seal, brick red or pink nose leather and paw pads.

Blue Tortie Tabby Point Bluish-white body. Points colour has blue tabby markings mingled with cream tortie markings. Nose rims are blue-grey. Nose leather is blue-grey, old rose or pink. Paw pads are blue-grey and/or pink.

OPPOSITE and OVERLEAF
The Balinese is every bit as graceful and elegant as its Siamese cousin, as this Chocolate Point demonstrates.

Chocolate Tortie Tabby Point Ivory body. Points colour has milk chocolate tabby markings mingled with red tortie markings. Nose rims are chocolate. Nose leather is milk chocolate, pale red or pink. Paw pads are cinnamon to milk chocolate and/or pink.

Lilac Tortie Tabby Point Glacial white body. Points colour has lilac tabby markings mingled with cream tortie markings. Nose rims are lavender-pink. Nose leather and paw pads are faded-lilac and/or pink.

The ravishing Birman is a sociable animal and will tolerate children and other household pets quite happily.

BIRMAN

Origins First bred as a pedigree in France in the early 1920s, the beautiful semi-longhaired Birman was slower to gain popularity in the USA and the UK, where it was not recognized until the late 1960s. Various legends attempt to explain the ancestry of the Birman as originating from the temples of Burma (now Myanmar). However, the true origins of the breed are unknown.

Appearance The Birman's large body has thickset legs of medium length and short paws that end in distinctive white gloves. The head is broad and rounded, with full cheeks and a strong chin. Eyes are almost round and deep blue. The tail is medium-length and full. All Birmans have colourpointed features.

Coat The coat is long, silky and slightly curled on the belly, with a full ruff around the neck. All Birmans are colourpointed, with darker coloration on the ears, face, tail and legs. The coat is comparatively easy to keep well groomed with regular brushing and combing.

Characteristics and Temperament Birmans are proud, intelligent and inquisitive. They love people and are extremely loyal. Birman kittens are

58

particularly mischievous and their sense of fun stays with them into adulthood. They are also gentle and sensitive, and being sociable animals, will tolerate other cats and dogs quite happily. They quickly adapt to new surroundings, but have a tendency to pine if left alone for long periods of time.

Birman Varieties
Solid Point:
Eye colour for all varieties is blue.
Seal Point Pale fawn to cream body. Dark seal brown points, apart from the gloves, which are pure white. Dark seal brown nose leather and pink paw pads.
Blue Point Bluish-white body. Deep blue points except for the gloves, which are pure white. Slate nose leather and pink paw pads.
Chocolate Point Ivory body. Points are milk chocolate, except for the gloves, which are pure white. Cinnamon pink nose leather and pink paw pads.
Lilac Point Off-white body. Points are pinkish-grey, with pure white gloves. Lavender-pink nose leather and pink paw pads.
Red Point Creamy-white body. Points are a bright, warm orange, except for the white gloves. Pink nose leather and paw pads.
Cream Point Off-white body. Points are pastel cream. The gloves are white. Pink nose leather and paw pads.

LEFT
A Blue Point Birman.

Tortoiseshell and Tabby Point:

Seal Tortie Point Beige shading to fawn body. Points are seal brown patched with red. The gloves are white. Seal brown and/or pink nose leather.

Blue Tortie Point Bluish-white body. Points are blue-grey, patched with pastel cream. The gloves are white. Bluish-grey and/or pink nose leather.

Chocolate Tortie Point Ivory body. Points are milk chocolate patched with red. The gloves are white. Milk chocolate or pink nose leather.

Lilac Tortie Point Off-white body. Points are pinkish-grey mingled with cool-toned cream. The gloves are white. Pale pink or lavender-pink nose leather.

Seal Tabby Point Beige body. Points are dark seal tabby. The gloves are white. Brick red, pink or seal brown nose leather. Paw pads are pink.

Blue Tabby Point Bluish-white body. Points are blue-grey tabby. The gloves are white. Old rose or blue-grey nose leather.

Chocolate Tabby Point Ivory body. Points are milk chocolate tabby. The gloves are white. Light red, pink or milk chocolate nose leather.

Lilac Tabby Point Off-white body. Points are lilac tabby. The gloves are white. Lavender-pink or pink nose leather.

Red Tabby Point Off-white body with slight apricot tinge. Points are warm orange tabby. The gloves are white. Brick red or pink nose leather.

Cream Tabby Point Creamy-white body. Points are a darker cream tabby. The gloves are white. Pink nose leather.

Seal Tortie Tabby Point Beige body. Points have seal brown tabby markings mingled with red. The gloves are white. Seal, brick red or pink nose leather.

Blue Tortie Tabby Point Glacial white body. Points have blue tabby markings mingled with cream. The gloves are white. Nose leather is blue-grey, old rose or pink.

Chocolate Tortie Tabby Point Ivory body. Points have milk chocolate tabby markings, mingled with red and/or light red. The gloves are white. Nose leather is milk chocolate, pale red or pink.

Lilac Tortie Tabby Point Off-white body. Points have lilac tabby markings mingled with shades of cream. The gloves are white. Nose leather is lavender-pink and/or pink.

OPPOSITE, BELOW and OVERLEAF
The Birman has a large solid body, thickset legs and a medium-length bushy tail. White feet are also characteristic of the breed.

RIGHT, OPPOSITE and OVERLEAF

Maine Coons can grow to be quite large animals. They are also very lovable and make excellent family pets.

MAINE COON

Origins This is one of the oldest natural breeds in North America and has been recognized as a true variety for well over 100 years. The breed originated in the state of Maine on the north-eastern side of the USA. The name 'coon' arose because it was once thought that the cat was the product of matings between domestic cats and racoons – although this is not biologically possible. A more romantic theory suggests that Marie Antoinette sent her cats to America during the time of the French Revolution, and these became the ancestors of the breed. The more likely explanation is that the Maine Coon resulted from matings between local domestic cats and longhaired cats introduced by sailors visiting coastal towns. A Maine Coon won the Best in Show award at the 1895 Madison Square Gardens Show, but the breed did not achieve wide international recognition until the 1980s. In fact, it faded from the cat scene in its homeland in the early 1900s, as breeders preferred to show more exotic cats, such as Persian Longhairs, which were introduced to the USA from Europe at this stage.

Appearance A handsome, sturdy, medium to large cat. The head has a

gently concave outline when viewed in profile, with a squared-off muzzle. The nose is of medium length. Eyes are large and slightly oval, and the colours may range from green, blue and hazel to copper. The large ears are wide at the base and set well apart on the head. The tips of the ears bear small tufts of fur. The Maine Coon has a long, muscular and well proportioned body with medium-length legs and large, round paws. The impressive tail should be nearly as long as the body.

Coat These are semi-longhaired cats with heavy, shaggy fur. It tends to be

Black Dense coal black coat. Black nose leather. Black or brown paw pads.
Blue Grey-blue coat. Blue nose leather and paw pads.
Red Rich, brilliant red coat. Brick red nose leather and paw pads.
Cream Buff-cream coat. Pink nose leather and paw pads.
Tortoiseshell The coat is black with unbrindled patches of red and light red. A blaze of red or light red on the face is preferred.
Tortoiseshell-and-White Must have white on the bib, belly and all four paws. White on one-third of the body overall is preferred.
Blue-Cream Blue coat with clearly defined, unbrindled patches of cream on the body and extremities. Points are seal brown patched with red. Seal brown and/or pink nose leather and paw pads.
Blue-Cream-and-White There must be white on the bib, belly and all four paws. White on one-thrid of the body overall is desirable.
Bi-Colour Solid colour and white. Coloured areas predominate, with white areas located on the face, chest, belly, legs and feet. Colours accepted are black, blue, red and cream.

Smoke and Shaded Varieties:
Any solid or tortie colour is accepted.

The Maine Coon has a thick, dense coat designed to keep it warm in a cold climate. They come in many varieties, but tabby is the most common. Here we have a traditional tabby and a red tabby.

thicker and longer around the back, sides and belly, but there should also be a full frill around the neck, although this is lost when much of the longer hair is moulted in the spring, being a feature associated with the winter coat. The fur on the tail should be long and flowing. Many colours are recognized in the breed; tabby patterns are common.

Characteristics and Temperament
Although large, these cats are sweet-natured, friendly animals. Both attractive and amusing in their antics, they are considered by many to be the ideal pet cat. They are slow to mature

and may take up to four years to attain full adult stature.

Typical Maine Coon Varieties
The coat must be solid to the roots and free from shadings, markings or hair of another colour. Patterning should cover the coat, including the legs and tail in tortoiseshells. In bi-colours and parti-colours, any solid, tortoiseshell, tabby, shaded or smoke colour is accepted, combined with white.

Solid and Parti-coloured Varieties:
White Glistening white coat. Pink nose leather and paw pads.

The base coat should be as White, with the tips of the hairs shading to the basic colour. The Smoke is densely coloured, while the Shaded shows much more of the silver undercoat.

Shaded Silver White undercoat with a mantle of black tipping shading down the sides, face and tail. Colour ranges from dark on the ridge to white on the chin, chest, stomach and undersides of the tail. The legs are the same tone as the face. Eye rims, lips and nose are outlined with black. Brick red nose leather. Paw pads are black.

Shaded Red White undercoat with red tipping shading down the sides, face and tail. Colour ranges from dark on the ridge to white on the chin, chest, stomach and underside of the tail. Legs are the same tone as the face. Black nose leather and paw pads.

Black Smoke The white undercoat is deeply tipped with black. Points and mask are black, with a narrow band of white at the base of the hairs. The frill and ear tufts are light silver. Black nose leather and paw pads.

Blue Smoke The white undercoat is deeply tipped with blue. Points and mask are blue, with a narrow band of white hairs next to the skin. The frill and ear tufts are white. Blue nose leather and paw pads.

Red Smoke White undercoat deeply tipped with red. Points and mask are red, with a narrow band of white hairs next to the skin. Rose eye rims, nose leather and paw pads.

Cream Smoke A dilute version of the Red Smoke, in which the red tipping is reduced to pale cream.

Tabby Varieties:
Both the Classic Tabby and Mackeral Tabby patterns are accepted in the following colours:

Silver Tabby Silver base coat with dense black markings. Brick red nose leather. Paw pads are black.

Brown Tabby Coppery-brown base coat with dense black markings. Backs of the legs from paw to heel are black. Black or brown nose leather and paw pads.

Red Tabby Red base coat with deep, rich-red markings. Brick red nose leather and paw pads.

Blue Tabby Pale bluish-ivory base coat with deep blue markings. Old rose nose leather. Paw pads are rose.

Cream Tabby Pale cream base coat with buff or cream markings. Pink nose leather and paw pads.

Cameo Tabby Off-white base coat with red markings. Points colour has blue tabby markings mingled with cream tortie markings. Rose nose leather and paw pads.

Tortie Tabby (or Torbie) Silver or brown tabby with patches of red and light red. Brick red or pink nose leather. Paw pads are black and/or pink.

Blue Tabby Blue with patches of cream. Blue and/or pink nose leather and paw pads.

Tabby-and-White Any tabby colour as defined above, with or without white on face, but with white on the bib, belly and paws. White on one-third of the body is preferred. Nose leather and paw pads are coloured as above.

Tortie Tabbie-and-White Colour as for Tortie Tabby, but with white markings typically on bib, belly and paws. Colours are silver, brown and blue. Nose leather depends on basic colour. Paw pads are pink

ABOVE
This striking Maine Coon has a solid blue coat.

OPPOSITE
Three tabby kittens.

The Norwegian Forest Cat has an ancient heritage and may have arrived in Norway from Turkey a long time ago. Here we have a Cream-and-white, a Black Smoke, a Tabby-and-white, and (opposite) a Black-and-white.

NORWEGIAN FOREST CAT

Origins Though its origins are unknown, it is possible that the Norwegian Forest Cat can trace its ancestry back to longhaired Turkish cats, which had arrived in Norway by around AD1000 with Viking traders from the East. For centuries, the 'Wegie' was used as a working cat on Scandinavian farms. It was not until the 1930s that it was taken seriously as a breed, and planned breeding did not begin until the 1970s. The first Wegies arrived in the USA in 1979 and in Britain in the 1980s, since when the breed has established a strong international following.

Appearance Its long, strongly built body and long hind legs give the Wegie a solid bearing. The cat's head is triangular with a long, straight profile, and the ears are pointed and erect. The eyes are large and open and the chin is firm. The tail is long and bushy and the paws are tufted.

Coat The Wegie's double-layered coat grows heavier during winter to keep out both cold and wet. A woolly undercoat keeps the body warm, while a smooth, water-repellent upper coat keeps out rain and snow. The generous frill of fur at the neck and chest is likely to be shed during the summer months.

Characteristics and Temperament The Wegie is generally alert and active. It can be very playful while retaining the independent character of its semi-wild forbears. It is affectionate but dislikes being cosseted and will defend its territory vigorously. It is a superb climber and hunter, and has even been known to fish in streams! This cat must not be confined indoors.

Typical Norwegian Forest Cat Varieties In Norwegian Forest Cats, there is no

Norwegian Forest Cats love their home comforts, but must never be confined. They enjoy their freedom, defend their territory fiercely, and are excellent hunters.

relationship between the coat colour and eye colour, as found in most other pedigree breeds.

Solid Varieties:

White Glistening white coat. Pink nose leather and paw pads.

Black Dense coal black coat. Black nose leather and black or brown paw pads.

Blue Grey-blue coat. Blue nose leather and paw pads.

Red Rich red coat. Brick red nose leather and paw pads.

Cream Buff-cream coat. Pink nose leather and paw pads.

Tabby Varieties:

Silver Tabby Pale silver base coat with dense black markings. Brick red nose leather and black paw pads.

Brown Tabby Coppery-brown base coat with dense black markings. Black or brown nose leather and paw pads.

Blue Tabby Pale bluish-ivory base coat with deep blue markings. Old rose nose leather and rose paw pads.

Red Tabby Red base coat with deep rich-red markings. Red nose leather and paw pads.

Cream Tabby Pale cream base coat with buff or cream markings. Pink nose leather and paw pads.

Tabby-and-White Silver, brown, blue, red or cream. White on bib, belly and paws. Nose leather and paw pads as above.

RIGHT, OPPOSITE and
OVERLEAF
*Norwegian Forest Cats
have developed dense
coats to help them
withstand the freezing
Norwegian winters.*

Parti-Coloured Varieties:
Tortoiseshell Black coat with
unbrindled patches of red and light red.
A blaze of red on the face is preferred.
Tortoiseshell-and-White Colour as for
tortoiseshell, but there must be white on
the bib, belly and paws.
Blue-Cream Blue coat with unbrindled
patches of cream.
Blue-Cream-and-White Colour as for
Blue-Cream, but there must be white on
the bib, belly and paws.
Bi-Colour Combination of black, blue,
red or cream, and white. White areas are
on the face, chest, belly, legs and feet.

Smoke and Cameo Varieties:
Chinchilla White undercoat tipped
with black to give a sparkling silver
appearance. Chin, ear tufts, belly and
chest are pure white. Eye rims, lips and
nose are outlined with black. Black nose
leather and paw pads.
Shaded Silver White undercoat with a
mantle of black tipping down the sides,
face and tail. Colour ranges from dark
on the ridge to white on the chin, chest,
belly and underside of the tail. Eye rims,
lips and nose are outlined with black.
Brick red nose leather and black paw
pads.
Red Shell Cameo White undercoat,
sufficiently tipped with red to give a
sparkling appearance. Chin, ear tufts,

stomach and chest are white. Rose eye rims, nose leather and paw pads.

Red Shaded Cameo White undercoat with a mantle of red tipping down the sides, face and tail. Colour ranges from dark on the ridge to white on the chin, chest, belly and underside of the tail. Black nose leather and paw pads.

Black Smoke White undercoat deeply tipped with black. Points and mask are black. Frill and ear tufts are light silver. Black nose leather and paw pads.

Blue Smoke White undercoat deeply tipped with blue. Points and mask are blue. Frill and ear tufts are white. Blue nose leather and paw pads.

Red Smoke White undercoat deeply tipped with red. Points and mask are red. Rose eye rims, nose leather and paw pads.

RAGDOLL

Origins The world's largest domestic cat, the Ragdoll is a relatively new breed. Originating in California, the first steps towards creating it were rather muddled. A mitted Seal Point Birman male was mated with a non-pedigree longhaired white female. The resulting semi-longhaired kittens were cross-bred to produce the first pedigree Ragdolls. The first breeder coined the name Ragdoll because of the cat's tendency to go limp in people's arms. The Ragdoll has become a firm favourite in the USA and has been exported to Europe and Australasia.

Appearance The Ragdoll has a large build, with a medium to large head. The full cheeks taper to a well developed muzzle. The ears are medium-sized with rounded tips. The eyes are large and oval. The Ragdoll has a long, muscular body, medium legs and large, round paws. The tail is long and bushy.

Coat The Ragdoll's coat is semi-long, shorter around the head and longer towards the tail. The soft, silky texture makes it less prone to matting than the fur of many longhairs, and needs only moderate grooming. The coat is dark compared with other pointed breeds.

Characteristics and Temperament Ragdolls make good indoor pets, due to their placid nature. They don't need much exercise. Good news for wildlife-lovers is that Ragdolls do not seem to be interested in hunting. However, they are alert, intelligent and respond well to training. They love family life and get on well with children. They will tolerate being picked up and carried around – just like a rag doll, in fact.

Typical Ragdoll Varieties In all varieties the body is light in colour and only slightly shaded. The points (except the paws and chin) should be clearly defined, matched for colour, and in harmony with the body colour.

Mitted The chin must be white and a white stripe on the nose is preferred. White mittens on the front legs and back paws should be entirely white to the knees and hocks. A white stripe extends from the bib to the underside between the front legs to the base of the tail.
Seal Point Pale fawn to cream body. Dark seal brown points, except for white areas.
Blue Point Cold-toned bluish-white body. Blue points, except for white areas.
Chocolate Point Ivory body. Points are milk chocolate except for white areas.

OPPOSITE, LEFT and OVERLEAF
The Ragdoll is a charmer. It has a trusting and loving nature, so much so that it must be protected from danger. The name comes from the fact that the cats go limp like a 'ragdoll' when held.

RIGHT
Two Ragdolls: on the left, a Chocolate Tabby Bi-colour with a Blue-mitted Ragdoll on the right.

OPPOSITE
Two Seal Points.

Lilac Point Glacial white body. Points are pinkish-grey except for white areas.

Bi-Colour:
The mask has an inverted white 'V'. The belly is white and white legs are preferred. No white is allowed on the ears or tail.
Seal Point Pale fawn or cream body. Points are seal except for white areas.
Blue Point Cold-toned bluish-white body. Points are blue except for white areas.
Chocolate Point Ivory body. Points are milk chocolate except for white areas.
Lilac Point Glacial white body. Points are pinkish-grey except for white areas.

Colourpoint:
Seal Point Pale fawn or cream body. Dark seal brown points, except for white areas.
Blue Point Cold-toned bluish-white body. Blue points, except for white areas.
Chocolate Point Ivory body. Points are milk chocolate, except for white areas.
Lilac Point Glacial white body. Points are pinkish-grey, except for white areas.

Intelligent and resourceful, the Siberian Forest Cat can be aloof, but it is always loyal to its owner.

SIBERIAN FOREST CAT

Origins According to legend, the Siberian Forest Cats traditionally lived in Russian monasteries, where they patrolled the rafters on the lookout for intruders. Although fierce, the monks treated them as loving and loyal companions. It wasn't until the 1980s that a serious breeding programme to standardize the type was begun.

The Siberian Forest Cat has a thick dense coat, designed to help it cope in an unforgiving climate. It was once thought to have made its home in Russian monasteries, where it was cared for by monks in exchange for guarding the premises.

Although Siberians have been imported into the USA since 1990, so far TICA is the only major registry to recognize the breed.

Appearance This large, sturdily built cat has a broad head with a full, slightly rounded muzzle and a well rounded chin. The cat has large oval eyes and medium-sized ears with rounded tips. The inner ear has an abundance of ear tufts. The legs are thick and medium in length and the paws are large, round and tufted. The tail is medium length and thick, with a rounded tip. There is a tendency now for US bloodlines to be diverging somewhat in type from the

traditional appearance, becoming more rounded rather than angled like that of a wildcat. Siberian Forest Cats are bred in a wide range of colours and varieties, with tabbies, tortoiseshells and bi-colours being relatively common. Smokes and selfs are also seen.

Coat The top coat is strong, plush and oily to ensure that the cat can survive in the harshest conditions. The undercoat is dense enough to give excellent protection against the elements, becoming thicker in cold weather.

Characteristics and Temperament The Siberian Forest Cat is an active and highly agile animal that is also sensible and resourceful. Although friendly, it also maintains an independent side to its nature.

The handsome Siberian Forest Cat is bred in a wide range of colours and varieties, with Tabbies, Tortoiseshells, Bi-colours, Smokes and Selfs.

The Somali is a most elegant animal, with a lithe, muscular body and long legs ending in dainty oval paws. It is the Semi-Longhair version of the Shorthair Abyssinian.

SOMALI

Origins The Somali is closely related to the Abyssinian, of which it is the semi-longhaired version. Semi-longhaired kittens have occasionally appeared in the litters of the shorthaired Abyssinian over several decades.

At first, these kittens were discarded and given away as pets, but it was eventually realized that a new breed was making a spontaneous appearance. The long fur was probably the result of a naturally long-established recessive gene within the breeding population. Somali to Somali pairings produce all Somali kittens, although their coats are shorter at this stage than those of adults.

Appearance Its firm, muscular body is of medium build with long legs and a long tail with a full brush of hair. The paws are oval and tufted. Ears are tufted, too, and are large, cupped and wide-set. The head is a moderate wedge with a slight nose break in profile. The eyes are large, almond-shaped and wide-set.

Coat The coat is soft, fine and dense and lies flat along the spine. The pattern of the Somali's coat is ticked with as many as 12 bands of colour on each hair. It is easy to groom, though the ruff and tail need regular combing.

Characteristics and Temperament Not quite as outgoing as its Abyssinian relations, the Somali is nevertheless not suited to confinement to the house, and being a natural hunter it thrives on

activity. It is a charming and bright-eyed animal, with a cheeky demeanour, but is gentle and receptive to quiet handling and affection. It is soft-voiced and playful and makes a perfect companion pet.

Typical Somali Varieties

Although different cat associations have their own rules for acceptance of new varieties, the Somali is recognized in most of the regular Abyssinian colour varieties by most registration bodies.

Non-Silver Varieties:

Usual (Ruddy) The coat is a rich golden brown ticked with black. The tail is tipped with black. Ears are tipped with black or dark brown. The nose leather is tile red. Paw pads, heels and toe tufts are black or dark brown.

Blue Coat is blue ticked with darker blue.

Base hair is cream or oatmeal. Ears and tail are tipped with the same colour as the ticking. Nose leather and paw pads are blue-mauve. Toe tufts are deep blue.

Chocolate Coat is a rich coppery brown ticked with dark chocolate, with paler base hair. Ears and tail are tipped with the same shade as the ticking. Nose leather is a pinkish-chocolate. Paw pads are chocolate. Toe tufts are dark chocolate.

Lilac Pinkish dove grey coat ticked with a deeper shade of the same colour and a paler base coat. Ears and tail are tipped with the same colour as the ticking. Nose leather and paw pads are pinkish-mauve. Toe tufts are deep dove grey.

Sorrel Warm copper coat ticked with chocolate and a base coat of deep apricot. Ears and tail are tipped with chocolate. Nose leather and paw pads are pink. Toe tufts are chocolate.

Fawn Warm fawn coat is ticked with a deeper shade of the same colour and a paler base coat. Ears and tail are tipped with the same colour as the ticking. Nose leather is pink. Paw pads are pinkish-mauve. Toe tufts are deep fawn.

Silver Varieties:
A yellowish effect, known as 'fawning', is an undesirable trait in the Silver series of Somali cats. It occurs

particularly in the Usual Silver and Blue Silver varieties, especially on the face and paws.

Usual Silver White base coat ticked with black. Tail and ears are tipped with black. Nose leather is a light brick red. Paw pads are black or brown with black between the toes and black toe tufts.

Blue Silver White base coat ticked with blue. Ears and tail are ticked with blue. Nose leather and paw pads are blue-mauve with blue between the toes. Toe tufts are blue.

Chocolate Silver The white base coat has dark chocolate ticking. Nose leather is pinkish-chocolate and ears and tail are tipped with dark chocolate. Paw pads are chocolate with dark chocolate between the toes and ear tufts are dark chocolate.

Lilac Silver The white base coat is ticked with dove grey. Nose leather and paw pads are pinkish-mauve with dove grey between the toes. Toe tufts are dove grey.

Sorrel Silver The white base coat has chocolate ticking. Ears and tail are tipped with chocolate. Nose leather and paw pads are pink with chocolate brown between the toes. Toe tufts are dark chocolate.

Fawn Silver The white base coat is ticked with fawn. Ears and tail are tipped with fawn. Nose leather is pink. Paw pads are pinkish-mauve with fawn between the toes. Toe tufts are fawn.

OPPOSITE, LEFT and OVERLEAF
Somalis. These are quiet gentle cats which respond well to careful handling. They are excellent hunters and enjoy the outdoor life, so confinement is not an option for them.

The Tiffanie makes an affectionate and lively companion. It came about when a Lilac Burmese and a Chinchilla Longhair accidentally mated, the result being this extremely attractive cat.

TIFFANIE

Origins The Tiffanie came into being in the UK during the 1980s as a semi-longhaired version of the Asian group of shorthaired cats, and was first described as the Asian Longhair for a period. The origins of the breed can be traced back to an accidental mating between a Chinchilla Longhair and a Lilac Burmese. The first-generation offspring were shorthaired, shaded Burmillas, but subsequent breedings brought the recessive longhair and sepia pointing genes back to the surface. It is not the same as the Tiffany (now better-known as the Chantilly/Tiffany) breed created in the USA, whose origins at one stage were also thought to involve Burmese, in spite of the similarity in their names. The traditional colour associated with the Tiffanie is dark brown, but there are now an increasing number of combinations, including tabby variants and colours such as blue, lilac and cinnamon.

Appearance A medium-sized cat of which the females tend to be smaller than the males. Both are surprisingly heavy for their size. The head is rounded with a short nose and muzzle. The ears are quite large in relation to the head and set wide apart. Ear tufts are common. The eyes are large, wide-

set and slightly oriental. The legs are slender and in proportion to the body, and the paws are small and oval.

Coat The Tiffanie's coat is semi-long, fine and silky and longer at the ruff, which is quite pronounced. The cat sports a flowing, plume-like tail. The coat is quite easy to maintain with regular brushing.

Characteristics and Temperament The Tiffanie combines the traits of its parents' breeds to great advantage, being playful and affectionate with an extrovert nature. It is more lively than most Longhairs, but more docile than the Burmese. These cats make good pets.

99

The Turkish Angora has a gregarious nature and likes to chat in a very loud voice. It is spirited and intelligent and makes a lively and interesting companion.

TURKISH ANGORA

Origins Angoras from Turkey first reached France in the 1500s. While the Turkish cat was an essential ingredient in the creation of today's Longhaired Persian, its type was not as popular. By the early 1900s, cross-breeding with other longhaired cats had led to the virtual extinction of the breed outside Turkey, and even in its homeland it was scarce. A breeding programme was organized in Turkey by Ankara Zoo; then in the 1960s, the breed was imported into Sweden, the UK and the USA from Turkey. It has now been renamed the Turkish Angora to avoid confusion with the modern re-creation bred from Oriental stock in the UK, but early references in the 1900s to the Angora refer to this cat.

Appearance Graceful and athletic, the Turkish Angora is a small to medium-sized cat with a muscular body and attractively tapered head. The eyes are large and almond-shaped. In the White variety, one eye is often blue and the other green. The ears are long and pointed, well furred and tufted. The paws are small, round and dainty with tufts between the toes. The tail is long, tapering and bushy.

Coat The medium-length coat is fine and silky with no undercoat. The fur is wavy on the belly. Overall, it is relatively easy to groom with daily brushing and combing. These cats moult heavily in the spring and subsequently, Turkish Angoras

often resemble shorthaired cats through the warmer months of the year, but can still be distinguished by the longer fur on their tails.

Characteristics and Temperament The Turkish Angora is spirited with a sharp intelligence. It is often playful and enjoys games, but also likes peace and quiet. It is a companionable cat but can be aloof with strangers. It has a very loud voice and is an incessant talker. It can be destructive if left alone for any period of time.

Typical Turkish Angora Varieties
Eye colour is amber unless otherwise stated.
White Pure white coat. Pink nose leather and paw pads. There are three sub-varieties – Amber-eyed, Blue-eyed and Odd-eyed.
Black Dense coal black coat. Black nose leather and black or brown paw pads.
Blue Blue coat. Blue nose leather and paw pads.
Red Rich red coat. Brick red nose leather and paw pads.

The Turkish Angora played a large part in the creation of the Longhair Persian. The Angora itself was not always popular and almost became extinct with only a few remaining in Turkey until very recently. Thankfully, a breeding programme was established and the breed is now thriving.

Cream Buff-cream coat. Pink nose leather and paw pads.

Tortoiseshell Black coat with unbrindled patches of red and light red. A blaze of red on the face is preferred.

Blue-Cream Blue coat with unbrindled patches of cream..

Bi-Colour Combination of black, blue, red or cream, and white. White areas are on the face, chest, belly, legs and feet.

Calico A mostly white coat, with unbrindled patches of black and red, with white predominant on the underparts.

Black Smoke A white undercoat deeply tipped with black. Points and mask are black. Black nose leather and paw pads.

Blue Smoke A white undercoat deeply tipped with blue. Points and mask are blue, as are the nose leather and paw pads.

Tabby:
The following colours apply to both the Classic and Mackeral tabby patterns.

Silver Tabby Pale silver base coat with dense black markings. Brick red nose leather and black paw pads. Green or hazel eye colour.

Brown Tabby Coppery-brown base coat with dense black markings. Black or brown nose leather and paw pads.

Blue Tabby Pale bluish-ivory base coat with deep blue markings. Old rose nose leather and rose paw pads.

Red Tabby Red base coat with deep rich red markings. Red nose leather and paw pads.

The Turkish Angora has quite a long coat, so daily grooming is a necessity. Here we have a Blue Tabby (opposite), and a White (left).

The Turkish Van acquired its name from Lake Van in Turkey, where it was often seen swimming. Consequently, it has no objection to being bathed.

TURKISH VAN

Origins In 1955, two cats were brought to the UK from their native Lake Van area of eastern Turkey. The breed spread across Europe, but acceptance by registries took some time, eventually being achieved in 1969. Turkish Van cats were also introduced from Turkey directly to the USA, where they are now recognized by some associations.

Appearance A muscular cat with a long, sturdy body. The Turkish Van has a short, blunt, triangular head, a long, straight nose, and large, well-furred ears. The eyes are large, rounded and highly expressive. The legs are medium in length with neat, tufted, well rounded paws. The tail is a medium-length full brush in perfect proportion to the body.

Coat The Turkish Van has a long, incredibly soft, silky coat with no woolly undercoat. The pattern is predominantly white, with auburn or cream markings on the face, and a white blaze.

Characteristics and Temperament
Renowned as the Swimming Cat, due to its habit of taking a dip in the waters of Lake Van, the Turkish Van will swim if given the opportunity, and unlike many cats, has no objection to being bathed. It is self-possessed, affectionate and intelligent.

Typically, the Turkish Van has a predominantly chalk-white coat, with either auburn or cream markings. However, a number of other coloured markings are now acceptable, especially in the USA.

Typical Turkish Van Varieties
The two traditional colours are:
Auburn Chalk white coat. Auburn markings on the face with a white blaze. Eye rims, nose leather and paw pads are shell pink. Amber, blue and odd-eyed eye colour.
Cream Chalk white coat. Cream markings on face with a white blaze. Eye rims, nose leather and paw pads are shell pink. Amber, blue and odd-eyed eye colour.

In the USA, the CFA (Cat Fancier's Association) recognizes a much wider range of colour varieties in the case of the Turkish Van, including blue, black, tortie and tabby forms. However, research in Turkey suggests that the traditional favoured colour of these cats is actually pure white and free from any markings. Their odd-eyed appearance distinguishes them from the Turkish Angora breed, which originates from further west in the country. Yet the impact of the accepted Van patterning is such that it has now been developed in a number of other breeds, including Persian Longhairs. This has been achieved not by cross-breeding, however, but rather by selective breeding – choosing those cats whose patterning most closely resembles that of the Turkish Van, and developing the patterning in the breed from them.

SHORTHAIR GROUP

Oriental Shorthairs first became popular in the early 1960s when a small number of breeders began to mate Siamese with indigenous cats, such as the British, European and American Shorthairs, to produce a wide range of colours and coat patterns. They have since only been outcrossed to Siamese, so that they are temperamentally similar.

In the case of shorthairs, there is a noticeable difference between breeds originating from northern latitudes in Europe and those occurring nearer to the equator, which can be distinguished by having little undercoat. This is a reflection of the climate of their native environment, which is warmer and therefore means they need less insulation against the cold. As a result, their long outer guard hairs lie relatively smoothly, outlining the generally sleek profile of these athletic cats. It is also no coincidence that these breeds, evolved over the course of centuries, are smaller in size than those found in more northerly latitudes. It is easier for larger cats to maintain their core body temperature, thanks to their size, and this provides further evidence of how domestic cats have adapted relatively quickly to different environments.

The British Blue is probably the most popular of the British Shorthairs and is a good example of the type, being strong, robust and even-tempered. It has its ancestors in the first domestic cats that arrived in Britain with the Romans in the Ist century. The modern breed was developed in the 1880s, in response to the growing interest in showing cats which had begun at this stage.

The modern Abyssinian is possibly the ancestor of the ancient breed of cats revered by the Ancient Egyptians and depicted as the goddess Bast.

ABYSSINIAN

Origins This is one of the world's oldest cat breeds. First imported into the UK from Abyssinia (now Ethiopia) in Africa, as long ago as 1868, today's pedigree cats are not necessarily genetically linked to this individual. Its origins are, in fact, uncertain. Some claim that it was a Nile valley cat, worshipped by the ancient Egyptians. It certainly bears a close resemblance to the sacred cats carved and painted on Egyptian tombs. It also resembles the African wildcats, whose banded coats provide their owners with camouflage in the forest. Recognized as a breed in 1882, the Abyssinian was almost extinct in Britain at the start of the 20th century. Today, it is most popular in North America.

Appearance Medium size, slim and muscular. The head is slightly rounded and wedge-shaped, gently curved in profile. The American Abyssinian has a shorter head and a more rounded profile than its European counterpart. The nose is medium-length, the ears large, and the almond-shaped eyes are also large, and expressive. The tail is thick at the base and tapers.

Coat Soft, silky, fine-textured and medium-length. All Abyssinians have

Abyssinians are typical of most foreign breeds in that they are highly intelligent and have an extrovert personality. They are athletic cats and fond of inventing games.

unusual ticked coats, with two or three dark bands of colour in them. The ticking is also known as agouti, referring to a particular rodent whose hair has similar colour-banding down its length.

The earliest Abyssinians also showed tabby barring on their legs, but this has been removed over the generations by selective breeding, to the extent that the only evident tabby markings are now on the head, and the characteristic dark tip to the tail.

Characteristics and Temperament An active, intelligent cat that loves people; but it can be shy and mistrustful of strangers. It is, however, loyal and extremely affectionate towards its owners, though the Abyssinian tends to be more a climber than a lap-sitter. They are athletic and entertaining cats, fond of inventing games.

Typical Abyssinian Varieties
Ruddy (USA, Europe) **Usual** (UK-GCCF) The coat is ruddy-brown, ticked with darker brown or black with a deep apricot or orange-brown undercoat. The tail is tipped with black, the nose leather brick red. Paw pads and toe tufts are seal brown or black. The eye colour is gold or green.
Red or Sorrel The coat is a rich red ticked with chocolate brown. The

extreme outer tip is dark, with a red undercoat. The tail is tipped with chocolate brown. The nose leather is rosy pink. The paw pads are pink with chocolate brown toe tufts.

Blue The coat is beige, ticked with light cocoa brown; the extreme outer tip is the darkest, with blush beige undercoat. The tail is tipped with light cocoa brown. The nose leather is old rose. The paw pads are mauve, with slate-blue toes tufts.

Fawn The coat is rose-beige, ticked with light cocoa brown. The extreme outer tip is the darkest, with a blush-beige undercoat. The tail is tipped with light cocoa brown. The nose leather is salmon. The paw pads are pink with light cocoa brown toe tufts.

Black Silver The coat is silver-white, ticked with black, with a silver-white undercoat. The tail is tipped with black. The nose leather is brick red. The paw pads and toe tufts are black or seal brown. The shading is again most pronounced on the back and sides of the body, when compared with the underparts.

Blue Silver The coat is silver-white, ticked with dark steel blue-grey, with a silver-white undercoat. The tail tip and toe tufts are dark steel blue-grey. The nose leather is old rose. The paw pads are old rose or blue-grey.

The American Wirehair has a gregarious personality and a tendency to rule other cats with an 'iron paw'. They make good pets, however, as they are sturdy and adaptable and rarely destructive.

AMERICAN WIREHAIR

Origins The origins of the American Wirehair go back to a farm in Vermont, USA, in 1966. A red-and-white curly-coated male occurred as a spontaneous mutation in an American Shorthair litter. By 1969, a pure-breeding colony had been established and the breed was given official recognition by the CFA in 1977. The breed remains rare elsewhere in the world outside of the USA and Canada, but there was a class for American Wirehairs at a Brussels show in 1996.

Appearance A medium to large cat with a rounded head, prominent cheekbones and a well developed muzzle. The eyes are large, round, bright and clear. The American Wirehair comes in all colours and patterns except the colourpointed (Himalayan) series. In terms of type, the influence of the American Shorthair, which has been favoured as an outcross for this breed, is clearly apparent today.

Coat The unique, distinctive coat of the American Wirehair is springy, tight and medium-length. The individual hairs are thinner than usual, and crimped, hooked or bent. Stroking the fur feels rather like touching an astrakhan hat. A cat with curly whiskers is highly prized.

The American Wirehair is the result of a natural mutation from an American Shorthair. The coat is curly with an unusual springy texture, not unlike that of the Devon or Cornish Rex. Note the odd eyes of the white cat on the left of this page.

Minimal grooming is required, and an occasional soft brushing will keep the coat in top condition. The gentle use of a rubber brush will help to remove dead hair during a moult.

Characteristics and Temperament The American Wirehair is very positive and inquisitive, sometimes to the point of bossiness – indeed, it is said to rule the home and cats of other breeds with an 'iron paw'. However, it is also said to be a breed that never seems to stop purring! In addition, it is rarely destructive and enjoys being handled.

RIGHT, OPPOSITE and OVERLEAF

American Bobtails are almost dog-like in their behaviour. They enjoy carrying things around in their mouths and can open doors by standing up on their hind legs and turning the handle with their paws. They make devoted and enjoyable pets.

AMERICAN BOBTAIL

Origins The breed can be traced back to a random-bred bobtail kitten that was adopted from a Native American reservation by a couple from Iowa in the 1960s. The genetic antecedents of the breed remain unclear: however, both Manx and Japanese Bobtail genes may be present, as both completely tailless 'rumpies' and cats with shorter tails than normal, as well as individuals with tails of normal length, appear in the case of this breed. The American Bobtail was accepted for registration by the CFA in 2000, but only those cats with actual bobtails can be exhibited. The tail in this case should extend down to a point just above the hocks, and no lower.

Appearance A medium to large cat, the head is a broad, modified wedge, with a distinctive brow above large, almost almond-shaped eyes. Ears are medium with slightly rounded tips. The body is moderately long and the legs are in proportion to the body. The paws are large and round.

Coat The coat is resilient and resistant to water. The topcoat is hard with a soft undercoat that insulates the cat from extremes of weather. Grooming is minimal as the coat needs little or no brushing.

Characteristics and Temperament The American Bobtail is an extremely adept hunter and these instincts are satisfied in the home by catching flying insects in mid-air. These cats also like to stalk their toys and carry them in their mouths. Many American Bobtails are able to open doors by standing on their back legs and turning the doorknob with their paws. They bond well with their families and get on well with most dogs. Indeed, they are noted for their dog-like personalities and their devotion to their owners. They are excellent companions for children being, within reason, relatively tolerant of rough handling.

AMERICAN CURL

The American Curl has a pleasant and equable disposition and makes a good pet. It has a silky coat which comes in a variety of different colours and patterns.

Origins In 1981, a stray kitten appeared at a home in California, USA. The householder left food on the porch for it, which it ate, and adopted the house as its home. This female cat had a long, black, silky coat and very unusual ears

124

which curled back away from the face towards the back and centre of the head. Later that year, the cat had a litter of kittens, two of which had the same curled ears. These cats were shown in California in 1983 and the breed is now recognized in North America, the first American Curls reaching the UK in 1995. Outcrossing, which has produced a shorthaired Curl, ensures that genetic diversity continues to flourish within the breed. The curl itself has proved to be a dominant genetic trait, which means that kittens with ordinary ears born in a litter alongside American Curls will not carry the gene for this mutation, and are often described as Straight Ears. The curling causes these cats no apparent discomfort or problems.

Appearance The American Curl is a well balanced, moderately muscled cat that is slender rather than massively built. The head is a modified wedge with a rounded muzzle and firm chin. The ears are moderately large, wide at the base and open, curving back in a smooth arc when viewed from the front and rear. The ear tips are rounded. The eyes are walnut-shaped and slightly tilted. The paws are medium and rounded. The tail is equal to the length of the body, wide at the base, tapering and plumed.

Coat The coat is fine, silky and flowing with minimal undercoat. These cats can be bred in a very wide range of colours and patterns.

Characteristics and Temperament The American Curl is an alert and active cat with a gentle, even disposition.

The American Curl came about quite by accident, when a stray kitten appeared in California with strange curled ears and was subsequently bred to duplicate this unusual trait. In this case, the ears were folded backwards rather that forward as in the Scottish Fold Cat.

The difference between the American Shorthair and its British counterpart is negligible, although there are slight differences between American and British standards for the breeds.

AMERICAN SHORTHAIR

Origins The American Shorthair is very similar to British and European Shorthairs which are the oldest of the recognized shorthaired breeds. The breed's origins lie with the domestic cats taken to North America by settlers from Europe, dating back to the 1600s. At the beginning of the 20th century, some American breeders decided to develop this domestic cat's characteristics into a distinctive breed, as had happened in Europe with ordinary indigenous shorthairs. The first litter was from a mating of American and British Shorthairs. It was not until 1965 that the breed's name was changed from Domestic Shorthair to American Shorthair, in line with the names given to British and European Shorthairs.

Appearance A sturdy, medium to large cat with a strong, muscular body, and larger in size than an ordinary non-pedigree shorthair. The American Shorthair is not excessively cobby or rangy. The head is large with full cheeks and a square muzzle. The eyes are large, round, wide-set and slightly slanted. The legs are firm-boned and the paws firm, full and rounded with heavy pads. The tail is medium-length and heavy at the base, tapering to a blunt end.

The American Shorthair is healthy, hardy and robust and can grow to quite a large size. The breed has not spread significantly outside North America.

Coat The coat is short, dense, even and firm in texture. It is somewhat heavier and thicker in winter. Grooming is easy, with regular combing all that is required to keep the coat in good condition.

Characteristics and Temperament The American Shorthair is an easy-going, self-sufficient, no-nonsense cat. This even temperament ensures that the American Shorthair is an ideal family pet. It is bold, intelligent, inquisitive and active and prefers to have access to outdoors. It has proved to be both healthy and hardy. It gets on well with other breeds and with dogs, displaying a very adaptable temperament. Its similarity to British and European Shorthairs has meant, however, that the popularity of this breed has not spread significantly outside North America.

American Shorthair Varieties
Virtually all native European colours are recognized, reflecting the breed's heritage, but not colours and varieties of Asiatic origins, such as chocolate and lilac forms. Accepted colour forms include:
Self-Black A dense black coat with no markings or signs of rusting. Nose and paw pads are black.
Self-White A pure white coat with no markings.

Self-Cream A buff coat with no markings. Nose leather and paw pads are pink.

Bi-Colour The Black-and-White Bi-Colour should have a V-shaped blaze on the forehead with well defined patches of black, red, blue or cream on white.

Calico The classic Calico has patches of black and red on white. There are dilute versions of the colour combination available, in which the white feet, legs, chest, belly and muzzle are combined with even, unbroken patches of blue and cream.

Tortoiseshell A black coat patched with an unbroken area of red and cream. Eyes may be green or bright gold.

Tabby Varieties:

Blue Tabby Pale bluish-ivory base coat, lips and chin. The coat has very deep blue markings. The entire coat colour has warm fawn overtones. Nose leather is old rose, paw pads are rose, and eye colour is brilliant gold.

Brown Tabby Brilliant coppery-brown base coat with deep black markings. Lips and chin should be the same shade as the rings around the eyes. Nose leather is brick red, paw pads are black or brown, and eye colour is brilliant gold.

Red Tabby Red base coat, lips and chin, with deep rich red markings. Nose

OPPOSITE, LEFT and OVERLEAF
The American Shorthair comes in virtually all varieties, with the exception of Asiatic colours such as chocolate and lilac.

leather and paw pads are brick red. Eye colour is brilliant gold.

Cream Tabby Very pale cream base coat, lips and chin. Coat has buff or cream markings. Nose leather and paw pads are pink and eye colour is brilliant gold.

Cameo Tabby Off-white base coat, lips and chin. Coat has red markings. Nose leather and paw pads are rose and eye colour is brilliant gold.

Silver Tabby Pale, clear silver base coat, lips and chin. Coat has dense black markings. Nose leather is brick red, paw pads are black and eye colour is green or hazel.

Patched Tabby Similar to the established varieties of tabby but with the addition of patches of red and light red, or cream. Such cats are also described as Torbies, which is an abbreviation to describe their Tortoiseshell-Tabby patterning. As with other tortoiseshell variants, they are almost exclusively female, with males, when they do occur, being sterile.

Brown Patched Tabby Brilliant coppery-brown base coat, lips and chin. The coat has Classic or Mackerel markings of dense black and patches of red, sand or light red clearly defined on the body and extremities. A blaze of red or light red on the face is desirable. Lips and chin to be the same shade as the rings around the eyes. Eye colour is brilliant gold.

Blue Patched Tabby Pale bluish-ivory base coat, lips and chin. The coat has Classic or Mackerel markings of very deep blue and patches of cream clearly defined on both the body and the extremities. Warm fawn overtones suffuse the whole body. A blaze of cream on the face is desirable. Eye colour is brilliant gold or hazel.

Silver Patched Tabby Pale clear silver base coat, lips and chin. Coat has Classic or Mackerel markings of dense black and patches of red and/or light red clearly defined on both body and extremities. Warm fawn overtones suffuse the whole body. A blaze of red and/or light red on the face is desirable. Eye colour is brilliant gold or hazel.

BENGAL

Origins The Bengal is the result of the crossing of the Asian Leopard Cat with domestic cats in order to produce a wild-looking cat with a docile temperament. A rigid breeding programme was established in the 1980s to establish that the cat's wild tendencies had been bred out and that it was now suitable as a domestic pet. Early crosses were to non-pedigrees, but when the spotted leopard-like coat

The Bengal is reminiscent of wildcats, which was the intention when attempts to produce such a cat were begun in America in the early 1960s.

appeared, Bengals were crossed with Egyptian Maus and Ocicats. This practice is no longer condoned by most breeders.

Appearance Resembling a spotted Asian Leopard Cat, the Bengal is large, robust and muscular. The head is a medium wedge shape and rather small in proportion to the body. The profile has a gentle curve from the forehead to the bridge of the nose and a prominent brow. The nose is large and broad, and the eyes are large and almond-shaped. It has short ears.

Coat Unlike any other domestic cat, the Bengal's thick, luxuriant coat glitters as if sprinkled with gold dust. The silky texture is more like that of a wildcat's pelt than a domestic cat's fur. Bengals have been bred with both spotted and so-called marbled tabby markings, as well as Selfs.

Characteristics and Temperament A friendly, loving, alert, curious and intelligent cat, the Bengal has little fear of other cats, or any other animal. Bengals are not afraid of water. Indeed,

139

they like to play with it, and also with toys. They are great climbers and love heights.

Typical Bengal Varieties

Brown Tabby Reddish-brown with 'gold glitter' dusting and a yellow, buff, golden or orange undercoat. Markings are black or various shades of brown. There may be light-coloured spots on the backs of the ears, called ocelli. Whisker pads and chin are pale. Eye rims, lips and nose leather are outlined in black. The centre of the nose leather is brick red. Paw pads and tail-tip are black. Eye colour is gold, green or hazel.

Blue-Eyed Snow The coat is ivory to cream with pearl 'glitter' dusting. The pattern varies from charcoal to dark or light brown. Light-coloured spectacles, whisker pads and chin. Eye rims, lips and nose leather are outlined in black. The centre of the nose leather is brick red. Paw pads are a rosy-toned brown. Tail-tip is charcoal or dark brown. Eye colour is blue. This highly distinctive variant arose from the contribution of a pointed breed in the Bengal's ancestry, and has now become very popular.

Brown Snow The coat is cream to light brown with pearl glitter dusting. The pattern varies from charcoal to light brown. Light-coloured spectacles, whisker pads and chin. Eye rims, lips

OPPOSITE, LEFT and OVERLEAF
The Bengal is charming, intelligent and robust. It has been bred to have either a spotted leopard or a marbled tabby coat.

Bengals are playful cats which also enjoy water and climbing to great heights.

and nose leather are outlined in black. The centre of the nose leather is brick red. Paw pads are a rosy-toned brown. Tail-tip is charcoal or dark brown. Eye colour is gold, green or blue-green.

Blue The coat is a pinkish-mushroom to warm oatmeal with pearl glitter dusting. The pattern is pale blue to blue-grey. Light-coloured spectacles, whisker pads and chin. Eye rims, lips and nose leather are outlined in slate grey. The centre of the nose leather is dark pink. Paw pads are mauvish-pink. Tail-tip is dark blue. Eye colour is gold, green or blue-green.

The Bombay has a similar personality to the Burmese from which it was originally bred to produce a pure black cat.

BOMBAY

Origins The Bombay is named in honour of the Indian city of that name because of the resemblance the cat bears to the black panther – a native of India. In the 1950s, an American breeder tried to recreate the look of the panther by crossing black American Shorthairs and Sable Burmese. The Bombay was first recognized in the mid 1970s. In the UK, black British Shorthairs were mated with Burmese and became part of the Asian Group breeding programme.

Appearance The cat has a medium-sized, muscular body with a rounded head and full face. It has a short snub nose and a firm chin. The medium-sized ears have slightly rounded tips and are tilted slightly forwards, giving the cat an alert expression. The eyes are large, round and copper-coloured. The legs are in proportion to the body and the paws are round. Everything about the cat is black, from the nose to the paw pads.

Coat The short, shiny coat is very close-lying, with a sheen like jet black patent leather, hence the cat's nickname in America: 'the patent-leather kid with new-penny eyes'. The fur must be jet black to the tips. The coat needs very little grooming to keep it in top

condition; buffing with a silk scarf or velvet grooming mitt will enhance the coat's glossy sheen.

Characteristics and Temperament The Bombay has a typically Burmese temperament, being good-tempered – even sedate. But it is gregarious, affectionate and requires lots of attention. It makes a very good pet.

The Bombay is so-named because of its striking resemblance to the black panther of India.

The short, dense coat of the Bombay is so shiny that it resembles patent leather.

BRITISH SHORTHAIR

Origins This breed probably stems from
the first domestic cats that arrived in
Britain with the Romans in the Ist
century AD. The modern breed was
developed in the 1880s from farm, street
and domestic cats in the UK, in
response to the growing interest in
showing cats which began at this stage.
The breed was in decline by the turn of
the 20th century, however, due to the
rise in popularity of more exotic breeds
for show purposes, notably Persian
Longhairs, and had almost died out by
the 1950s. At that time, matings with
Blue Persians then resulted in the
British Shorthairs being developed in
terms of their size and appearance, and
helped them to regain their popularity.
Similar breeding programmes over
recent years have led to the introduction
of new colour variants to the breed,
such as Chocolate and Lilac, as well as
the creation of a Colourpoint lineage,
which combines the markings of the
Colourpoint Longhair (Himalayan)
breed with the appearance of the British
Shorthair. Nowadays, the British
Shorthair has become the third largest
group of registered pedigree cats in the
UK, thanks partly to the exposure which
the breed has received as a result of its
use in various advertising campaigns for
cat food.

Appearance The Shorthair's compact, well balanced and powerful body is surprisingly heavy. The chest is full and broad. Legs are short and strong with large, rounded paws. The tail is thick at the base and rounded at the tip. The head is very broad and round with well developed cheeks. The eyes are large and round, while the ears are small.

Coat The coat is short, thick and fine. Numerous guard hairs give the coat a distinctive, crisp feel. The protective undercoat insulates the cat from the cold. Daily grooming with a comb will keep the coat in prime condition, although, unlike the Longhair, this is not essential.

Characteristics and Temperament Its intelligent yet phlegmatic nature makes the British Shorthair a solid and dependable feline companion, responding readily to affection. It is also self-possessed and self-reliant, undemanding and friendly. The breed may appear to be a cuddly cross between a cat and a teddy bear, but they are also skilled hunters, and toms can be determined fighters due to their strong territorial instincts. Neutering will modify these aggressive tendencies towards other cats, but should not be carried out too early, before the

The British Shorthair has ancient origins and probably arrived in Britain with the Romans in the 1st century. The modern breed was developed in the 1880s through domestic, farm and street cats.

RIGHT
A British Shorthair Blue.

OPPOSITE
A Spotted Tabby.

distinctive fleshy pads, called jowls, have developed around the face. This creates what has been likened to a double-chinned appearance, which would otherwise not appear, as they only develop in mature toms.

Solid Varieties: These include
Black A jet black coat. Nose leather is black, paw pads are black or brown and the eye colour is gold, orange or copper
White A pure white coat. Nose leather and paw pads are pink. The Blue-eyed White has deep sapphire-blue eyes.
Orange-Eyed White This has deep orange, gold, or copper eyes, while the Odd-eyed White has eyes of different colours. Those Whites with blue eyes are likely to be afflicted by congenital deafness, with the weakness being confined to the side of the head with the blue eye, in the case of Odd-eyed Whites.
Cream A light cream coat. Nose leather and paw pads are pink and the eye colour is orange or copper.
Blue Light to medium-blue coat. Nose leather and paw pads are pink and the eye colour is gold, orange or copper.

Bi-Colour Varieties:
Colouring The coat can be any standard colour and white, including newer colours such as Chocolate or Lilac. Nose

This British Shorthair displays the classic Spotted Tabby markings. The spots can be round, oval or oblong and should be clearly defined, The letter 'M' should be clearly visible on the forehead.

leather and paw pads are generally pink or match that of the coat colour, or are sometimes a combination of the two. Ey colour is gold, orange or copper. Darker variants such as Black-and-White tend t be most popular, simply because they show greater contrast in their coats. Symmetrical markings tend to be most likely to catch the judge's eye, with the white areas in the coat typically comprising one-third to one-half of the total patterning.

Tortoiseshell Varieties
All of these are essentially female-only varieties, for genetic reasons. Although male cats will crop up occasionally, the will be infertile. This also applies in the case of Tortoiseshell-and-White varieties which are also sometimes known under their traditional name of Calico.

Tortoiseshell The coat is marked with black and both dark and light red. Colours should be brilliant, free from blurring, brindling and tabby patches, with no white markings. Nose leather and paw pads are pink and/or black. Eyes are gold, orange or copper.

Blue-Cream A blue coat with cream patches. Nose leather and paw pads are blue and/or pink and the eye colour is gold, orange or copper.

Chocolate Tortie The coat is a warm chocolate mixed with red and light red.

Colours should be brilliant, free from blurring, brindling and tabby patches, with no white markings. Nose leather and paw pads are pink and/or black. Eyes are gold, orange or copper.

Lilac Tortie The coat is marked with dark and light red and black, lilac and pale cream. Colours should be brilliant, free from blurring, brindling and tabby patches with no white markings. Nose leather and paw pads are pink and/or black. Eyes are gold, orange or copper.

Tortoiseshell-and-White Varieties:
Tortie-and-White The coat is equally balanced in light and dark red and black on white. No sign of brindling or tabby markings. There should be a white blaze down the face. Nose leather and paw pads are pink and/or black. Eyes are gold, orange or copper.

Blue Tortie-and-White The coat is equally balanced in light and dark red and black on white and patched with lilac and cream. No sign of brindling or tabby markings. There should be a white blaze down the face. Nose leather and paw pads are pink and/or black. Eyes are gold, orange or copper.

Tabby Varieties: Patterns:
Classic Tabby Markings should be dense and clearly defined. There are characteristic oyster-shaped blotches on the flanks. On the head, frown lines form a letter M and an unbroken line runs back from the outer corner of each eye.

Mackerel Tabby Markings should be dense and clearly defined and resemble narrow pencilling. In this case, a pattern of narrow dark lines resembling the skeleton of a fish radiate down the sides of the body from the central unbroken dark line running over the vertebral column. On the head, frown lines form a letter M and an unbroken line runs back from the outer corner of each eye.

LEFT
A handsome Cream Tabby.

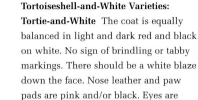

157

Spotted Tabby Clear round, oval, oblong or rosette-shaped spotting. The spots must be well defined, with the tail either ringed or spotted and terminating in a dark tip, in common with the other forms of tabby patterning. On the head, frown lines form a letter M and an unbroken line runs back from the outer corner of each eye.

Colours:

Brown Tabby A rich sable or brown coat with dense black markings. Lips and chin are the same colour as the rings around the eyes. Nose leather is brick red and paw pads are black or brown. Eye colour is gold, orange or green.

Red Tabby A rich red coat with dense black markings. Lips and chin are red. Nose leather and paw pads are brick red. Eye colour is gold, orange or green.

Silver Tabby A pale silver coat with dense black markings. Lips and chin are pale silver. Nose leather is brick red and paw pads are black. Eye colour is green or hazel.

Blue Tabby A pale bluish-ivory coat with dense blue markings. Lips and chin are a pale bluish-ivory. Nose leather is old rose and paw pads are rose. Eye colour is gold or copper.

Cream Tabby A pale cream coat with buff or cream markings. Lips and chin

OPPOSITE
Kittens in an assortment of colours.

LEFT
A British Shorthair orange-eyed White.

British Shorthairs make excellent companions. They are solid and dependable and respond well to affection.

are pale cream. Nose leather and paw pads are pink. Eye colour is gold or copper.

Other Varieties: These include **Black Smoke** The silver undercoat is tipped with black. Nose leather and paw pads are black. Eyes are gold or copper. **Blue Smoke** The silver undercoat is tipped with blue. Nose leather and paw pads are blue. Eyes are gold or copper. Where the markings at the tips of the guard hairs are less extensive, extending a shorter distance down the individual hairs, such cats are described as Tipped rather than Smoke.

Colourpointed The general type of this group of Shorthairs is the same for the British Shorthair. A range of points colours is accepted, ranging from Cream Point, being the lightest colour, through to Seal Point, which is the darkest. Variants including Tabby and Tortoiseshell forms have also been created, occurring both individually as Blue Tabby, for example, and in combinations such as the Seal Tortie Tabby, when red and cream patching is merged with the tabby patterning on the points.

BURMESE

Origins In the early 1930s, a Siamese hybrid female, named Wong Mau, was taken from Rangoon in Burma (now Myanmar) to the USA and mated with a Seal Point Siamese. Some of the resulting offspring were dark brown and formed the beginnings of the official pedigree Burmese. The breed was registered in 1936, and then in 1952 it was recognized in the UK. Since then, the breed has developed to slightly different standards on opposite sides of the Atlantic, with the result that there are now different classes at many cat shows in North America, catering separately for Burmese and also Burmese of European appearance.

Appearance Despite having a genetic pattern almost identical to the Siamese, the Burmese is much more compactly built, not having been subsequently evolved on such extreme lines. In fact,

The Burmese has a sunny nature and keen intelligence. Its playfulness remains with it throughout its life.

The Burmese is a result of a mating between a hybrid Siamese and a Seal Point Siamese, resulting in offspring that were dark chocolate-coloured, and which formed the basis of the Burmese breed.

hese cats approximate more closely in ype to early Siamese, compared with heir contemporary cousins. The nose has an obvious break in its line. The head is round with very full cheeks. The eyes are large, round and yellow to gold n colour. The cats have well proportioned legs and neat, oval paws.

The tail is straight and of medium length, tapering to a rounded tip. Those of US origins are more cobby in shape, a fact emphasized by their legs, which are slightly shorter than those of their European counterparts, which have a more angular profile overall, and oval-shaped eyes.

Coat The short, fine, glossy coat is close-lying and needs very little grooming to keep it in top condition.

Characteristics and Temperament The Burmese has a sunny disposition and keen intelligence. It is active, inquisitive and adaptable. However, it does not like

165

RIGHT, OPPOSITE and
OVERLEAF
*The Burmese is similar
in stature to the
Traditional Siamese
(page 366), being stockier
and with more rounded
features than the modern
Siamese.*

being left alone and can be strong-willed. It is less vocal and demonstrative than other Oriental breeds. These cats remain playful all their adult lives and need a devoted human family surrounding them.

Solid Varieties:

Red Light tangerine coat. Ears are darker than the body. Nose leather and paw pads are pink. Eye colour is yellow to gold.

Cream Pastel cream coat. Ears are darker than the body. Nose leather and paw pads are pink. Eye colour is yellow to gold.

Sable The warm, sable brown coat shades to a lighter tone on the underparts. Nose leather and paw pads are brown. Eye colour is yellow to gold.

Blue Soft silver-grey coat, slightly darker on the back and tail. There is a silver sheen on the ears, face and feet. Nose leather and paw pads are blue-grey. Eye colour is yellow to gold.

Chocolate Warm milk chocolate coat. Nose leather is chocolate brown and paw pads are cinnamon to chocolate brown. Eye colour is yellow to gold. Often known in North America as the Champagne.

Lilac The pale dove grey coat has a pinkish tone. Ears may be darker than the body. Nose leather and paw pads are

lavender-pink. Eye colour is yellow to gold. Breeders often refer to these cats as Platinum Malayans in North America, with the description of 'Malayan' being favoured for the newer Burmese coat colours by some cat organizations there.

Tortoiseshell Varieties:

Seal Tortie Seal brown, red and/or light red, patched and/or mottled. Nose leather and paw pads are plain or mottled, seal brown and/or pink. Eye colour is yellow to gold.

Blue-Cream Tortie Pale tones of blue and cream, patched and/or mottled. Nose leather and paw pads are plain or mottled, pink and/or blue-grey. Eye colour is yellow to gold.

Chocolate Tortie Milk chocolate, red and/or light red, patched and/or mottled. Nose leather and paw pads are plain or mottled, milk chocolate and/or light red or pink. Eye colour is yellow to gold.

Lilac-Cream Tortie Lilac and pale cream, patched and/or mottled. Nose leather and paw pads are plain or mottled, pale pink and/or lavender-pink. Eye colour is yellow to gold.

BURMILLA

Origins An accidental mating between a lilac Burmese female and a Chinchilla Silver male in 1981 resulted in the birth of attractive shaded-silver female kittens. They were all of shorthaired Burmese type with the stunning tipping and outlined features of the Chinchilla.

Similar matings were carried out and in 1983, the Cat Association of Great Britain accepted breeding programmes and a standard of points for the breed to be known as Burmilla. Kittens are paler in colour than adults, while Shaded colours have darker coats than Tipped varieties.

Appearance The female Burmilla is markedly smaller and daintier than the male, but the body type is generally medium-sized and straight-backed. Legs are long and sturdy with neat, oval paws. The Burmilla carries its tail high and proud. The head is a medium wedge, gently rounded at the top and

the ears are large. The large, expressive eyes are outlined with dark 'eyeliner'. The lips and nose leather are similarly outlined. The tail is medium to long, fairly thick at the base and tapering slightly to a rounded tip.

Coat The coat is short, dense, soft and glossy, slightly longer than the Burmese and with enough undercoat to give it a slight lift. The Burmilla's most impressive feature is the sparkling shading or tipping on the coat. It is best to groom the dense coat with a rubber brush to loosen dead hairs before combing.

Characteristics and Temperament The Burmilla is stable and dignified, but inquisitive and sociable, too, though less boisterous than the typical Burmese. However, they are more sociable than Longhairs. They are playful and very affectionate.

Burmilla Varieties:
Black Shaded or Tipped Pure silver-white coat, shaded or tipped with black. Nose leather is brick red. Paw pads and soles are black. Eye colour is green.
Blue Shaded or Tipped Pure silver-white coat, shaded or tipped with blue-grey. Nose leather is brick red. Paw pads and soles are blue-grey. Eye colour is green.

The Burmilla is the result of a mating between a Burmese and a Chinchilla. It is an attractive cat with a proud bearing.

Brown Shaded or Tipped Pure silver-white coat, shaded or tipped with dark brown. Nose leather is brick red. Paw pads and soles are dark brown. Eye colour is green.

Chocolate Shaded or Tipped Pure silver-white coat, shaded or tipped with milk chocolate. Nose leather is brick red. Paw pads are chocolate tinged with pink and soles are chocolate. Eye colour is green.

Lilac Shaded or Tipped Pure silver-white coat, shaded or tipped with lilac. Nose leather is brick red. Paw pads are lavender-pink and soles are grey tinged with pink. Eye colour is green.

Red Shaded or Tipped Pure silver-white coat, shaded or tipped with red. Nose leather is pink. Paw pads are pink and soles are red. Eye colour is green or amber.

Cream Shaded or Tipped Pure silver-white coat, shaded or tipped with pale cream. Nose leather and paw pads are pink. The soles are red. Eye colour is green or amber.

Red Tortoiseshell Shaded or Tipped Pure white coat, shaded or tipped with a patchwork of red and black. Nose leather and paw pads are black, pink, or mottled black-and-pink. The soles are black and/or red. Eye colour is green or amber.

OPPOSITE and LEFT
The Lilac-tipped Burmilla has a luxurious coat which appears tinged with silver and is made all the more striking by the cat's black-rimmed, intense green eyes.

Blue Tortoiseshell Shaded or Tipped
Pure white coat, shaded or tipped with a patchwork of blue-grey and cream. Nose leather and paw pads are blue-grey, pink, or mottled blue-grey-and-pink. The soles are blue-grey and/or red. Eye colour is green or amber.

Brown Tortoiseshell Shaded or Tipped
Pure white coat, shaded or tipped with a patchwork of dark brown and red or light red. Nose leather and paw pads are dark brown, pink, or mottled dark brown-and-pink. The soles are dark brown and/or red. Eye colour is green or amber.

Chocolate Tortoiseshell Shaded or Tipped Pure white coat, shaded or tipped with a patchwork of milk chocolate and light red. Nose leather and paw pads are chocolate, pink, or mottled chocolate-and-pink. The soles are chocolate and/or light red. Eye colour is green or amber.

Lilac Tortoiseshell Shaded or Tipped
Pure white coat, shaded or tipped with a patchwork of lilac and cream. Nose leather and paw pads are lavender-pink, pink, or mottled lavender-pink-and-pink. The soles are grey tinged with pink. Eye colour is green or amber.

OPPOSITE
A Brown Shaded Burmilla.

LEFT
A Brown Shaded kitten. Burmilla kittens are much paler in colour than adults.

Because it is a genetic combination of the boisterous Burmese and the more sedate Chinchilla, the Burmilla's temperament strikes a happy medium. They are quietly dignified, but also like a game and make affectionate pets.

RIGHT, OPPOSITE and
OVERLEAF
The Chartreux is a rather
quiet but affectionate cat.
Similar in looks to the
British Shorthair Blue, it
is nevertheless smaller in
stature. It has a thick
and luxurious silver-blue
coat which requires
regular grooming to keep
it looking its best.

CHARTREUX

Origins Native to France, this breed is said to have been bred as long ago as the 16th century near the French town of Grenoble, at the Monastery of La Grande Chartreuse (which was also responsible for the liqueur of that name). In the 1930s, a French vet suggested that the breed should have its own scientific name. The Chartreux reached North America in the 1970s, but is not bred in many European countries. This breed should not be confused with the British Blue or the European Shorthaired Blue.

Appearance Well proportioned but stocky, with short legs and large, muscular shoulders, the Chartreux is rather lighter than its British counterpart, the British Blue Shorthair. Its head is large and round with well developed cheeks and a short, strong neck. Eyes are large and open, not too rounded, and with the outer corners slightly uptilted. Eye colour is vivid deep yellow to vivid deep copper. Ears are medium-sized and set high on the head. The paws are large and the tail is medium-length with a rounded tip.

Coat The coat is dense, soft and plush with a slightly woolly undercoat and a glossy appearance. Daily grooming with a comb is needed to keep the undercoat

n good condition, while brushing nhances the way in which the coat haracteristically stands away from the ody.

Characteristics and Temperament A calm, affectionate, intelligent and attentive cat. It is less talkative than most breeds, with a high-pitched miaow and an infrequently used chirp. The cat will happily live confined to the house, so it is a suitable pet for an apartment-dweller.

179

The Cornish Rex, like the similar Devon Rex, are both natural mutations, bred to duplicate the recessive, distinctive curly coat.

CORNISH REX

Origins The first recorded Cornish Rex kitten was born in 1950 in Cornwall, England. The kitten, named Kallibunker, was red with a white chest and belly and its fur was closely waved. It was mated with its mother, and the resulting litter contained two curly-coated kittens. Descendants were then backcrossed to Rex cats to create the recessive curly coat. The breed was officially recognized in 1967 in the UK and 1979 in the USA.

Appearance The Cornish Rex is medium-sized, hard-bodied, muscular and slender, with a curving back and huge ears set high on a disproportionately small head. The arched back is set on fine, lean legs. The American standard for these cats requires a 'tucked-up' torso that gives the cat the appearance of a whippet.

Coat The most unusual feature of the Cornish Rex is its short, plush, regularly-waved coat. Because it lacks guard hairs, the coat is soft and velvety to touch. The whiskers and eyebrows are crinkled. The curly coat does not shed hair, making it easy to groom by stroking.

Characteristics and Temperament Affectionate and people-oriented, the Cornish Rex wags its tail to show that it

is happy. These cats are very lively,
playful and agile, capable of leaping
effortlessly from ground to shoulder
height. They enjoy games of fetch, catch
and batting objects with their paws.

RIGHT, OPPOSITE and OVERLEAF
Because it lacks guard hairs, the coat of the Cornish Rex is soft and velvety to the touch and can be groomed merely by stroking it. The cats are fine-limbed, with a slim body, small head and large ears.

Cornish Rex Varieties
To widen the gene pool and ensure stamina in the Cornish Rex as a breed, the first breeders outcrossed to other breeds that had the desired conformation. Foreign breeds, such as the Havana, Russian Blue, Burmese and Siamese were selected, especially in North America, whereas British Shorthairs were used for this purpose in the UK. All the offspring of Cornish Rex and non-rexed cats resulted in cats with normal coats. All carried the recessive gene for the curly coat and when these cats matured and were mated, approximately half the litter on average would be comprised of curly-coated kittens. The various colours and coat patterns of the cats selected for the original outcrosses resulted in a wide range of colour varieties in the Cornish Rex breed, and breeders soon began to show their preferences for certain colours and combinations of colours.

The Devon Rex loves people and is very demanding of attention. It also loves playing the fool and has boundless energy. However, it is not the ideal pet for everyone.

DEVON REX

Origins In 1960, in Devon, England, a curly-coated feral male was mated with a stray, straight-haired female. The litter included one curly-coated male, named Kirlee, showing that the curly hair gene was recessive. The parents were almost certainly related, and inbreeding was needed to perpetuate the Devon Rex. By 1970, the breed had been recognized in the UK. It was not until 1979 that it was recognized in the USA.

Appearance The Devon Rex shares the muscular build, slim legs and long, whip-like tail of the Cornish Rex, but it is broad-chested, and has a flat forehead, prominent cheekbones and a crinkled brow. Its coat runs in a rippled pattern

rather than wavy like the Cornish Rex, which is a quite separate mutation, in spite of both breeds arising in neighbouring counties in the south-west of England. The face of the Devon Rex is wide with large, round eyes, prominent, brittle whiskers and huge, low-set ears. These cats are commonly nicknamed 'poodle cats' because of their wavy coats and habit of wagging their tails. The Devon has a quizzical impish expression, which some people regard as almost extraterrestrial.

Coat The Devon Rex coat is generally less dense and more coarse and curly than that of the Cornish Rex and, without careful breeding, very sparse coats can result. Kittens in particular often have relatively sparse coats. Even the whiskers are affected and, being crinkled, tend to break more easily than normal. The coat requires gentle stroking with a soft mitt rather than a brush. A piece of silk is often favoured by exhibitors of Devon Rexes to give a good gloss to the coat. All coat colours, patterns and colour combinations are allowed in the case of this breed.

Characteristics and Temperament This is certainly a cat for the connoisseur. Even more playful than the Cornish Rex, the Devon Rex loves fooling around. It

The Devon Rex shares many of the attributes of the Cornish Rex, except that it is slightly stockier with a wider head and a wrinkled brow.

can be extremely mischievous and demanding of human attention, but is extremely loving and intelligent.

Rexed Coats
There are a number of different types of rex, with the Cornish and Devon Rexes being the most popular today. Their coats differ, however, in that in the case of the Devon Rex, all three types of hair are present in the coat, whereas the Cornish Rex lacks the outer guard hairs, and the secondary hairs and underlying down are shorter than normal as well. However, these are not as curled as in the Devon Rex. While the rex feature is most commonly associated with short coats, it can also be seen in longhaired cats, such as the La Perm (page 235) and the Selkirk Rex (page 276), which also exists in a corresponding short-coated form.

Despite controversy as to its actual ancestry, the Egyptian Mau is essentially a breed developed in America, where it has been developed into the cat we know today. Right is a Black Smoke, while far right and opposite is a Bronze.

EGYPTIAN MAU

Origins Not only can images of a spotted tabby cat be seen in the wall paintings and scrolls of ancient Egypt, but its descendents may still be seen on the streets of Cairo today. Many believe that the Egyptian Maus are direct descendents of the African wildcats that they more closely resemble than any other domestic cat. Maus were probably introduced into Europe aboard the ships

A Black Smoke kitten.

of Phoenician traders more than 2,000 years ago. The current stock in the USA is descended from three Maus imported into the USA in the 1950s by an exiled Russian princess.

Appearance The Egyptian Mau is medium-sized, long and graceful, with a head that is a slightly rounded wedge-shape. The medium to large ears are alert and slightly pointed and the inner ear is a delicate shell pink. Legs are in proportion to the body and the paws are small and slightly oval. The tail is thick at the base and slightly tapered.

Coat The coat is short and silky with random spots that vary in size and shape. The spots form a contrast to the lighter background coat that comes in just three colours: Silver, Bronze and Black Smoke. The hair has two or more bands of ticking, separated by lighter bands. The coat is easy to maintain but needs regular grooming.

Characteristics and Temperament
These cats are alert, affectionate and intelligent, but rather shy. The Egyptian Mau is good with children but dislikes

The Egyptian Mau is thought to be an ancient breed, as striking spotted tabbies, similar to this, can be seen in ancient artefacts. Here is a Silver Mau.

The coat of the Silver Egyptian Mau has a pale silver base with dark grey/black markings which contrast dramatically with its gooseberry-green eyes.

strangers. It is happiest given plenty of space for jumping, climbing and hunting.

Egyptian Mau Colours

Of the three traditional colour forms, the Bronze is the most ancient-seeming. Markings on the flanks are random, but spots along the spine run in symmetrical lines, often joining into a dorsal stripe at the start of the tail.

Silver Pale silver ground colour with dark charcoal markings that contrast with the base colour. The backs of the ears are greyish-pink, tipped with black. The nose, lips and eyes are outlined in black. The upper throat, chin and around the nostrils is a pale clear silver appearing white. Nose leather is brick red. Paw pads are black and the eye colour is a light gooseberry green.

Bronze Light bronze ground colour with creamy ivory underparts and dark brown markings that contrast with the base colour. The backs of the ears are a tawny pink tipped with dark brown. The nose, lips and eyes are outlined in dark brown, with ochre on the bridge of the nose. The upper throat, chin and around the nostrils is a pale, creamy-white. Nose leather is brick red. Paw pads are black or dark brown. The eye colour is a light gooseberry green.

Black Smoke This has a charcoal grey ground colour with a silver undercoat and jet black markings clearly visible against the base colour. The nose, lips and eyes are outlined in jet black. The upper throat, chin and around the nostrils are lightest in colour. The nose leather and paw pads are black. The eye colour is a light gooseberry green.

OPPOSITE
The Silver Mau is strikingly elegant.

LEFT
A Bronze Egyptian Mau.

The European Shorthair is an active cat which enjoys its independence. It doesn't respond too well to being confined to the house.

EUROPEAN SHORTHAIR

Origins The first European Shorthairs were descended from cats introduced to Northern Europe nearly 2,000 years ago by Roman soldiers, who brought them to kill rats in their food stores. Until 1982, European Shorthairs were classified with British Shorthairs. FIFe then gave the breed its own category and it began effectively as a ready-made breed, with a full range of colours, established type and breeding stock, with known histories. The breed is now being

A Non-Silver Tabby kitten.

selectively bred, this trend having started in Scandinavia, and no British Shorthair crosses are now being permitted in the pedigree of these cats, nor are Persian Longhairs, used in the past to increase the size of the breed. It is not recognized by the GCCF or major breed registries outside Europe.

Appearance More elegant than the British Shorthair, emphasis in the European Shorthair lies in its lithe muscularity rather than round cobbiness. Its face is slightly longer and less heavily jowled than its British cousin's. The body is strong and broad-chested, with fairly long, well boned legs and firm, rounded paws. The tail is in proportion to the body and rounded at the tip. Largish ears are upright with rounded tips and set fairly wide apart. The eyes are large, round and well spaced.

Coat The all-weather coat is short and dense, with a crisp texture. It stands away from the body. Grooming is easy. Regular brushing to keep the undercoat in good condition is all that is necessary.

Characteristics and Temperament The European Shorthair is particularly adaptable, independent and bright, and

The European Shorthair was introduced to northern Europe by Roman soldiers, where it was used to protect grain stores from rodents. The breed later combined with the British Shorthair, but in recent years has been given a status of its own. It is more elegant than the British Shorthair.

therefore must not be confined indoors. It is also placid and affectionate and relatively quiet, thus making it an ideal family pet.

Typical European Shorthair Varieties: White All three sub-varieties of the European Shorthairs must have pure white coats. The first sub-variety has

deep blue eyes; the second has green, yellow or orange eyes; the third, the White Odd-eyed, has one blue eye and the other either green, yellow or orange.

RIGHT
*Black and Bi-colour
European Shorthair
kittens.*

OPPOSITE
*A Non-Silver Tabby
adult.*

RIGHT
*The Black Tortie Smoke
has green, yellow or
orange-coloured eyes –
most striking in a dusky
face.*

OPPOSITE
A Non-Tabby Bi-colour.

Selfs Black, blue, red or cream body. Eye colour is green, yellow or orange. No tabby markings permitted, although these may be apparent initially in kittens.

Tortie variants The body is patched with either black and red, for the Black Tortie, or blue and cream for the Dilute or Blue-cream Tortie. For both, the eye colour is green, yellow or orange. Tortie-and-White forms also exist.

Smoke White or silver undercoat. Varieties include Black Smoke, Red Smoke, Blue Smoke, Cream Smoke.

Black Tortie Smoke and Blue Tortie Smoke All have either green, yellow or orange eyes.

Non-Silver Tabby Coat pattern is Blotched (known as Classic), Mackerel or Spotted. Varieties include Black Tabby, Blue Tabby, Red Tabby, Cream Tabby, Black Tortie Tabby and Blue Tortie Tabby.

Silver Tabby Markings are etched on a base colour of pure pale silver. There should be no ticked hairs or brindling in the pattern. Three tabby patterns – Classic, Mackerel and Spotted – are accepted. The varieties include Black Silver Tabby, Blue Silver Tabby, Red Silver Tabby, Cream Silver Tabby, Black Tortie Silver Tabby and Blue Tortie Silver Tabby. Eye colour is green, yellow or orange.

Non-Tabby Bi-Colour Van, harlequin and bi-colour patterns are accepted. Markings may be black, blue, red, cream, black tortie or blue tortie. In van and harlequin, eye colour may be deep blue, green, yellow or orange, or odd-eyed with one eye deep blue and the other green, yellow or orange. In the bi-colour pattern, eyes may be green, yellow or orange.

Van-Patterned White coat with two coloured patches on the head, separated by a white blaze down the nose. Nose leather is pink.

Tabby Van A white coat with patches of any of the three basic tabby patterns on the head, separated by a white blaze down the nose. Nose leather is pink or pinkish-red, outlined with the appropriate colour for the patterned areas.

Tortie Van White coat with patches of any of the three basic tortie patterns on the head, separated by a white blaze

down the nose. Nose leather is patched with pink. Another female-only variety, like all torties.

Harlequin White with solid-coloured patches over at least a quarter, but not more than half, of the body. Coloured parts should consist of patches surrounded by white. Tabby and Tortie Harlequins are also accepted. Nose leather is as for the van pattern.

Bi-Coloured White with coloured parts which must be clearly separated from each other. At least half, but not more than two-thirds, of the cat must be coloured. Coloured parts must be evenly distributed.

Tabby Bi-Colour Classic, Mackerel and Spotted varieties. The Tortie Bi-Colour should have large, well-defined patches of clear, bright colours. Nose leather is as specified for the Van pattern.

OPPOSITE
A Red Tabby.

LEFT
This Black Tortie Tabby has Mackerel markings.

EXOTIC SHORTHAIR

Origins The breed was developed in th
mid 1960s, with the aim of producing a
shorthaired Persian cat. Thus Persians
were crossed with various shorthairs an
the product was a shorthaired cat that
required minimal grooming and had the
Persian's gentle nature. It has all the
physical characteristics of the Persian c
and is available in the same colours and
variations. Some Exotic Shorthairs have
also inherited the defects of the Persian
so in North America, only outcrosses
with American Shorthairs and Persians
are allowed. Elsewhere, other breeds m
sometimes be used.

Appearance The Exotic Shorthair is of
medium to large build and cobby. The
head is round and massive and set on a
short, thick neck. The cat has full cheek
and broad, powerful jaws. The eyes are
large, round and bright. The nose is sho
and stubby, and the ears are small and
blunt, set wide apart and leaning slight
forward.

Coat The coat is not quite short but no
semi-long either. It is slightly longer tha
other shorthairs' but not long enough to
flow. The texture is dense, plush, soft
and lively. It is not flat or close-lying.
Grooming is easy, though thorough
brushing and combing a couple of time

Having been bred from the Persian, the Exotic Shorthair has inherited the placid nature of that breed. It is quite a sedate cat and will happily live indoors as a family pet. Here is a Cream-and-White.

OPPOSITE
A Blue-Cream kitten.

a week is necessary. Shining fur is achieved by correct feeding. The coat occurs in all colours found in American Shorthairs and Persians.

Characteristics and Temperament The Exotic Shorthair has the placidity and dignity of the Persian, yet also has a playful and affectionate side to its nature. It is patient with children and is content to be an indoor cat. It has the soft, squeaky voice of its parent breed.

Typical Varieties:

White A pure glistening-white coat with pink nose leather and paw pads. Eye colour is deep blue or brilliant copper. Odd-eyed Whites should have one blue and one copper eye of equal colour intensity. Deafness is again associated with blue eyes in these cats.

Black Dense coal black coat with black nose leather and black or brown paw pads. Eye colour is brilliant copper.

Blue An even tone of blue stretches from the nose to the tip of the tail. Blue nose leather and paw pads. Eye colour is brilliant copper.

Red Deep, rich, brilliant red coat with brick red nose leather and paw pads. Eye colour is a brilliant copper.

Cream An even shade of buff-cream coat with pink nose leather and paw pads. Eye colour is brilliant copper.

The Exotic Shorthair was developed by crossing Persians with American Shorthairs and other shorthaired breeds. The result is a shorthaired Persian-type cat which nevertheless has a slightly longer coat than the traditional Shorthair.

213

RIGHT
*A Silver Tabby Exotic
Shorthair.*

OPPOSITE
*The Blue Exotic
Shorthair is literally blue
from its nose to the tip of
its tail. The eye colour is
brilliant copper.*

Chocolate A warm-toned, medium to dark chocolate coat with chocolate nose leather and paw pads. Eye colour is copper or orange.

Lilac A warm-toned lilac coat with lilac nose leather and paw pads. Eye colour is copper or orange.

Tabby and Bi-Colour Varieties:

Classic and Mackerel Patterns The following colours are all recognized: silver, brown, blue, chocolate, lilac, red and cream.

Tortie Tabby Brown, blue, chocolate and lilac colours are allowed.

Bi-Colour The coat is white with unbrindled patches of either black, blue, red or cream. Nose leather and paw pad colour corresponds with the basic coat colour. Eye colour is brilliant copper.

Van Bi-Colour A white coat with unbrindled patches of either black, blue, red or cream confined to the head, tail and legs.

Van Blue-Cream and White White coat with unbrindled patches of both blue and cream confined to the head, tail and legs.

Other Varieties:

Tortoiseshell Black coat with clearly defined, well broken, unbrindled patches of red and light red on the body and extremities. A red or light red blaze on

the face is desirable. Eye colour is brilliant copper.

Tortie-and-White White coat with unbrindled patches of red and black, with white predominant on the underparts. Eye colour is brilliant copper.

Blue-Cream (Dilute Tortie) Blue coat with clearly defined, well broken patches of unbrindled solid cream on the body and extremities. Eye colour is brilliant copper.

Blue-Cream-and-White White coat with unbrindled patches of blue and cream, with white predominant on the underparts. Eye colour is a brilliant copper.

Chinchilla Pure white undercoat. Coat on the back, flanks, head and tail is tipped with black to give a sparkling silver appearance. Chin, ear tufts, stomach and chest are pure white. Rim of eyes, lips and nose are outlined with black. Nose leather is brick red, paw

pads are black. Eye colour is green or blue-green.

Shaded Silver Pure white undercoat; topcoat is heavily shaded with black to form a mantle over the spine, sides and on the face and tail, creating a darker impression than in the case of the Chinchilla. Legs are the same tone as the face. Rims of the eyes, lips and nose are outlined with black. Nose leather is brick red, paw pads are black. Eye colour is green or blue-green.

Chinchilla Golden The rich, warm-cream undercoat and the coat on the back, flanks, head and tail is tipped with seal brown to give a golden appearance. Chin, ear tufts, stomach and chest are cream. Rims of eyes, lips and nose are outlined with seal brown. Nose leather is deep rose, paw pads are seal brown. Eye colour is green or blue green.

Shaded Golden The rich, warm-cream undercoat and coat is heavily shaded with seal brown to form a mantle over the spine, sides and on the face and tail, which is darker than in the Chinchilla Golden. Legs are the same tone as the face. Rims of the eyes, lips and nose are outlined with seal brown. Nose leather is brick red, paw pads are seal brown. Eye colour is green or blue green.

Tipped The tipping may be of any colour accepted in the Persian varieties. The undercoat must be as white as possible and the tip of each hair lightly coloured, giving a sparkling effect. The nose leather in cats with black tipping is brick red, and in all other colours to correspond with the coat colour. Paw pads in the Black Tipped may be either black or seal brown, in other colours, to correspond with the coat colour.

Smoke There is darker shading than in the case of the Tipped. May be of any colour accepted in the Exotic Group, but instead of being sound in colour from the tips to the root of the coat, the base of each hair is silvery-white. No tabby markings are allowed. Nose leather and paw pads should correspond with the coat colour. Eye colour is copper, orange or deep gold.

Colourpointed This has a pale body and colour on the points. There must be a good contrast between the body and points colour, although kittens are pale at birth and only develop their coloration relatively slowly. Points should be free from white hairs. Nose leather and paw pads should correspond with the individual points' colour. Eye colour is blue.

OPPOSITE
A Silver tabby Exotic Shorthair.

LEFT
A red-and-white Bi-colour Exotic Shorthair kitten.

Shaded Tortoiseshell The white undercoat and coat is heavily shaded with black tipping and clearly defined patches of red and light red hairs, as in the pattern of the Tortoiseshell, to form a mantle over the spine, sides and on the face and tail. Nose leather and paw pads are black, pink or mottled.

The Havana Brown is an intelligent, lively and active cat, and thrives on plenty of love and attention.

HAVANA BROWN

Origins For a hundred years, breeders had been trying to develop an all-brown cat. In the 1950s, British cat breeders developed a solid chocolate of Siamese type from the accidental mating of a black non-pedigree cat and a Chocolate Point Siamese. The colour was called Havana, but the breed was registered in the UK as the Chestnut Brown Foreign Shorthair, being known under this name until the 1970s. Havana Browns were also exported to the US. They were registered as Havana Browns until 1973, when the CFA accepted the Oriental Shorthair breed. From then on these imports were registered as Chestnut Oriental Shorthairs. The unusual description of Havana was chosen because of the striking similarity between the colour of these cats and that of the rabbit breed which was already known by this name.

Appearance The head is shaped like the Siamese's, being longer than it is wide. The ears are large and round and slightly pricked to give an alert appearance. The oval eyes are a vivid green. The body is medium-sized, firm and muscular and the medium-length tail tapers gently to a slightly pointed tip. The males are usually larger than the females. All Havana Browns are a

For many years, breeders had been trying to produce an all-brown Oriental. Happily, this happened by chance when a Chocolate Point Siamese was mated with a black non-pedigree cat. The result is this beautiful cat.

warm chestnut brown colour. There is now a distinct difference in appearance between these cats in North America and Europe, with those of North American origins having a less extreme appearance, with a more rounded head-shape than their European counterparts. This is because Siamese have not played such a significant role in their development.

Coat The coat is short to medium in length, smooth and lustrous, and is easy to maintain with the minimum of grooming. Combing will remove any loose hairs.

Characteristics and Temperament A highly playful, athletic and energetic cat, fond of games and an excellent climber, the Havana Brown is a sweet-

natured and sociable cat. It thrives on plenty of affection and attention. These cats are highly intelligent and like investigating new things, pawing and playing with objects. It is less vocal than a Siamese and makes an excellent pet.

The Japanese Bobtail is friendly and curious and often raises a paw as if in greeting.

JAPANESE BOBTAIL

Origins This is a breed that has existed in Japan for many centuries. The Japanese Bobtail is considered to be a symbol of domestic good fortune and probably originated from domesticated shorthaired cats that had mutated into a tailless version. It was not until after World War II that the Bobtail was discovered by the international cat fancying world. In 1963, American judges visiting a show in Japan,

spotted a Bobtail, and were impressed. Five years later, an American breeder took 38 Bobtails back to the USA from Japan and the breed became accepted for show purposes in 1978 by the CFA. The breed is also now recognized in the UK, but is virtually unknown there at present.

Appearance The Japanese Bobtail's distinctive tail is just 3–4-in (8–10-cm) long. It is normally curled up in a bob, but can be held upright when the cat is alert or advertising its presence. The body is medium-sized, slim but well muscled. The head is pointed, with high cheekbones and slanted eyes that

roduce a unique profile. The Bobtail is available in most colours and patterns. In Japan, the Van-patterned Tortie-and-White, known as *Mi-ke* (meaning three colours) is the most prized. There is also a long-coated version of this breed, which was recognized separately from its short-coated counterpart in the USA during 1991. These particular cats appear to be naturally more common in northern parts of Japan, with their tails resembling fluffy pompoms.

Coat The coat is medium in length, soft and silky with no undercoat and little shedding of hair. Grooming is easy with regular combing.

Characteristics and Temperament
Friendly, curious and playful, and being very people-oriented, Bobtails make ideal family pets. They often have an endearing habit of raising one paw as if in greeting. They have a soft voice with a range of sounds. Bobtails enjoy swimming and can also be taught to retrieve.

RIGHT, OPPOSITE and
OVERLEAF
*The Japanese Bobtail has
existed in Japan for
many centuries and is
said to bring good
fortune to the home.
They probably originated
from mutations of
ordinary domesticated
cats to the breed we see
today.*

The Korat has a forceful personality and is quite demanding and attention-seeking. However, they are very playful and respond well to training.

KORAT

Origins Alongside the Siamese, the Korat is one of the distinctive cats of Thailand, and is considered a good-luck charm in its native land. A pair of Korats is a traditional wedding present, intended to bestow long life, wealth and happiness. Known since at least the 14th century, it is described in the *Cat Book of Poems*, a 16th-century manuscript of the ancient Thai kingdom of Ayutthaya. In the 20th century, Korats captured the attention of US servicemen in Thailand, and the first examples of the breed were imported into the USA in 1959. It gained official recognition in 1966, but was not introduced into Europe until 1972.

Appearance A strikingly handsome cat with large and piercing green eyes which are round and prominent when open, but appear slanted when closed. The Korat's head is large and heart-shaped, giving it a soft appearance. The chin is firm and rounded. The ears are large with rounded tips, set high on the head, giving the cat an alert expression. The Korat's body is well muscled and strong. Blue of a silvery shade is the traditionally accepted colour form in the West, although recently, odd lilac Korats have been bred in Europe, cropping up unexpectedly in litters of ordinary Korats. In the UK, these cats are officially described as the Thai Lilacs of Korat Type, following a ruling by the GCCF in 1998, although they are not yet recognized for show purposes.

Coat The glossy, fine, close-lying coat is short, with no undercoat. The coat is blue, with the guard hairs tipped in

Along with the Siamese, the Korat is the other distinctive cat of Thailand, where it is considered lucky. It is reputed to bring long life, wealth and happiness.

The Korat is a beautiful cat with a well muscled, athletic build. It usually has a rich blue coat, which in certain lights can appear silver, and striking green eyes.

lver, giving it an intense sheen.
rooming is minimal. A cloth or comb
n over the coat is all that is needed to
eep it smooth.

Characteristics and Temperament
These cats have a strong personality and
can be demanding. They like to have
their own way and need plenty of

attention. They are extremely playful
and respond well to training.

La Perm is a breed which
is virtually unknown
outside the US. It can be
shorthaired, when the
coat, eyebrows and
whiskers have a distinct
curl, or longhaired when
ringlets form in the coat.
They are sociable cats
and enjoy human
companionship.

LA PERM

Origins In 1986, on a farm in Oregon, USA, a litter of six kittens was born to a farm cat. One of the kittens was born bald. Within eight weeks, the kitten began to grow very soft, curly hair. By four months, it had a full coat of curly hair. It was later mated and gave birth to five male kittens, all bald at birth, like their mother had been. As the breeding programme progressed, it became clear that the curly gene was dominant and could be carried by both males and females. The owner gave the cats the breed name 'La Perm', signifying wavy or rippled. Of the major registries, only TICA and the CFA have recognized the breed, this status first being accorded to the breed in 1995. Interestingly, today's La Perm kittens are not normally bald at birth, which could have served to lessen their chances of survival by leaving them more vulnerable to becoming chilled. Nevertheless, the breed still remains essentially unknown outside North America.

Appearance The face and head is somewhat triangular in shape with wide-set ears, relatively large whisker pads, and large, expressive eyes. La Perms can also boast a splendid set of curly whiskers and eyebrows.

Coat The coat can form waves or ringlets that range from tight to long corkscrew curls, depending on whether the cat is short- or long-coated. The coat generally stands away from the body, parting down the middle. Grooming is minimal because the coat does not easily mat. Because of the appearance of its coat, the breed is still sometimes known as the Alpaca Cat, the alpaca being a relative of the shaggy-coated llama, highly prized for the quality of its wool.

Characteristics and Temperament La Perms are gentle and affectionate but also very active. However, unlike many energetic breeds, these cats are also content to be lap cats. They seek human contact and will purr as soon as they see you, making them probably the most sociable breed of all. Generally they are quiet, but they can be vocal when seeking attention.

The Manx is quiet, calm and intelligent and would rather be safely asleep by the fireside than gadding about outside.

MANX

Origins This unusual cat with no tail hails from the Isle of Man, UK. The lack of a tail, however, is a genetic mutation that occurs occasionally in all animals. In isolated populations, such as on islands, there is a greater chance that such a gene will be perpetuated. The original mutation must have occurred many years ago, for Manx cats have been known for a long time to a specialist breed club first established in Britain in

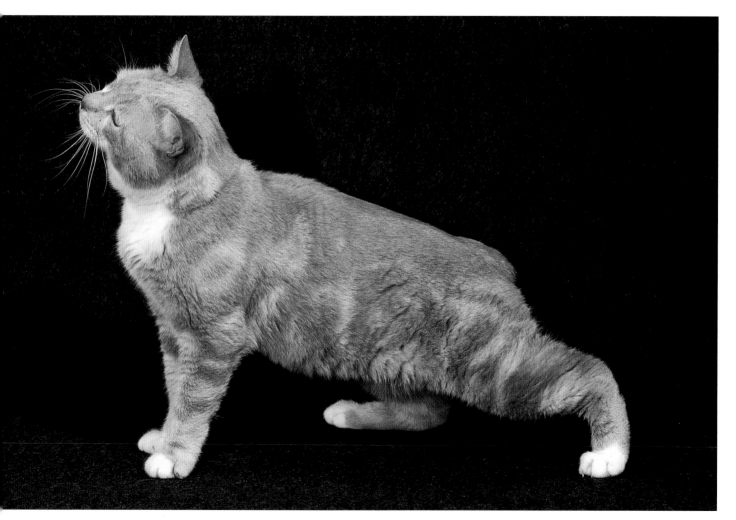

The Manx comes from The Isle of Man in the Irish Sea off the west coast of Britain. It has no tail, which is a natural mutation that can occur in any animal. However, because of the smallness of the Isle of Man, the mutant gene has been perpetuated.

RIGHT, OPPOSITE and OVERLEAF

The Manx comes in four types, but the Rumpy, which has a slight hollow on the rump where the tail should be, is the only acceptable form for showing.

1901. Although it is an old breed, Manx cats remain rare. Breeders have to cross tailless Manx with Manx that have tails as there is a lethal genetic factor involved in Rumpy-to-Rumpy pairings, which will cause some of the kittens to die at or shortly after birth.

Appearance The breed's most obvious characteristic is its frequent lack of a tail and rounded body shape. The only acceptable form for showing is the Rumpy, in which there is a slight hollow

n the rump where the tail should be. There are also three recognized varieties with residual tails of varying lengths. The Rumpy Riser has only a vestigial knob for a tail, the Stumpy has a short tail, while the Longy has a shortened but otherwise normal tail. Manx cats also have a distinctive 'bunny-hop' gait, caused by the lack of a tail combined with hind legs that are longer than the front legs.

Coat The Manx's coat is short, dense and double, giving a padded quality due to the comparatively long, open outer coat and the close, cottony undercoat. Regular grooming is essential.

Characteristics and Temperament These cats are affectionate, calm, quiet and intelligent. They are not particularly active and prefer sitting with their owner to being out of doors.

Manx Varieties
The Manx is accepted in the following colour varieties by most American associations: Black, Blue, Red, Cream, Tortoiseshell, Blue-cream, Calico, Dilute Calico, Chinchilla, Shaded Silver, Black Smoke, Blue Smoke; Classic and Mackerel Tabby in the following colours: Brown Tabby, Blue Tabby, Red Tabby, Cream Tabby, Cameo Tabby, Silver Tabby; Patched Tabby in Brown, Blue and Silver.

*Two Rumpy Manx cats:
right, a Tabby and
opposite a Tortoiseshell
(Calico).*

The Cymric is an offshoot of the Manx and came about when certain Manx females had longhaired kittens. Cymric comes from Cymru, *meaning Wales.*

CYMRIC

Origins In the late 1960s, breeders of Manx cats in North America discovered that long-coated kittens occasionally appeared in the otherwise normal litters o their Manx queens. It was decided to develop them as a separate breed in their own right. The name Cymric (pronounced koom-rik) is derived from *Cymru*, which i the Welsh word for Wales. The breed was thus named in honour of the Principality, which was said to have its own variety of tailless cats. The breed is recognized by some associations, but not in the UK and apart from the coat, has the same standar requirements for show purposes as the Manx cat. The CFA in the USA now describes these cats simply as the Longhaired Manx (see previous pages).

Appearance A semi-longhaired version a Manx cat, the Cymric appears in the same Rumpy, Rumpy Riser, Stumpy and Longy versions.

Coat The coat is silky with hard guard hairs which are uneven in length, giving padded, heavy look to the body. The san coat colours and patterns are accepted a for the Manx.

Characteristics and Temperament Like the Manx, the Cymric is affectionate, intelligent and extremely loyal, and like to be with its owner.

The Ocicat is an amiable cat; it loves people and gets along well with other animals. It also has an outgoing personality and enjoys climbing and exploring the great outdoors.

OCICAT

Origins The first kitten of this breed appeared in the 1960s as the result of the accidental mating of a hybrid Abyssinian-Siamese female with a Chocolate Point Siamese male. The spotted pattern of the kitten reminded its breeder's daughter of a baby ocelot, and she decided to produce similar cats which were eventually recognized as a separate breed called the Ocicat. It obtained full championship status in North America in 1987. A similar breeding programme has seen the Ocicat being created on similar lines in Europe, where it is currently growing in popularity.

Appearance The Ocicat is a rather large, but well proportioned cat, powerful and agile with a typical 'wildcat' appearance. The head is wedge-shaped with clear, definite markings including the characteristic tabby M on the forehead. It has a broad muzzle and strong chin. The ears are

RIGHT, OPPOSITE and
OVERLEAF
*The Ocicat appeared in
the 1960s as the result of
an accidental mating of a
hybrid Abyssinian-
Siamese female with a
Chocolate Point Siamese
male. The resulting
kittens had spotted coats
reminiscent of ocelots,
hence the name Ocicat.*

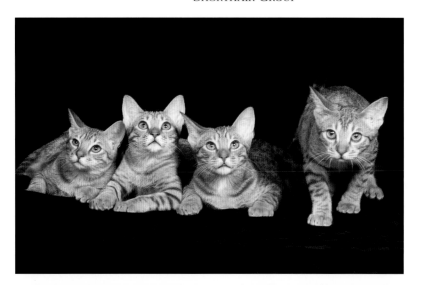

large and alert. The Ocicat is remarkable
for its striking, almond-shaped eyes. The
long body is athletic and muscular, the
legs are long and the tail fairly long and
slightly tapered. Originally, the number
of Ocicat colours was restricted, but
more colours were introduced by
crossing examples of the breed with
American Shorthairs. The range of
colours now includes Chocolate, Blue,
Lavender and Fawn, as well as Silver
and Smoke variants.

Coat The Ocicat's coat is short and
smooth, satiny and lustrous. All hairs,
except those on the tip of the tail, are

banded. Hairs in the ground colour are
tipped with a lighter colour. The patte...
is that of a spotted tabby cat, although
the spotted patterning becomes less
obvious during a moult. The tail shou...
always end in a dark tip, reflecting the
true coat colour of the individual.
Gentle brushing is all that is required ...
way of grooming.

Characteristics and Temperament
Ocicats are loving and gentle,
inquisitive and playful, and make
excellent pets. They are outgoing and
are friendly towards strangers and eve...
dogs. They love to explore their
surroundings and need plenty of
opportunity for climbing.

The Ocicat is a large, powerful and agile cat, and its striking, almond-shaped eyes and rich dense coat with spotted markings gives it the appearance of a wildcat.

The Oriental is a demanding cat and likes plenty of attention. However, it can be endearing as it is extremely affectionate and will run to greet its owner rather like a dog.

ORIENTAL SHORTHAIR

Origins Oriental cats first became popular in the early 1960s when a small number of breeders began mating Siamese with indigenous cats, such as the British, European and American Shorthairs, to produce a wide range of colours and patterns. They have since only been outcrossed to Siamese. The care taken with the selection of their foundation stock ensures strength, stamina and good temperament, as well as beauty. This is one of the most diverse of all cat breeds and groups.

Appearance By and large, Oriental cats are identical to Siamese cats in all respects except for having all-over coat colour and pattern rather than the Siamese colourpoints on face, ears, tail and legs. Unlike the Siamese, most Orientals do not have blue eyes. Their appearance is almost canine – moving as they do like a whippet, and with a whip-like tail.

Coat The Oriental cat's coat has a short, fine texture that is glossy and close-lying. They are naturally very clean cats and minimal grooming is required. Buffing with a soft glove or silk scarf is recommended.

Characteristics and Temperament This is an extrovert cat, intelligent, inquisitive, and very affectionate. It is

ctive and playful and hates being left
[al]one for long periods. The Oriental is as
[ta]lkative as a Siamese, but its voice is a
[li]ttle quieter. Many people find that the
[ca]t's response to humans is much like
[th]at of a dog. Orientals will often run to
[gr]eet their owners on their return home,
[an]d demand to be played with.

[Or]iental Varieties

[So]lid Varieties:

**[Or]iental White, Foreign White, Siamese
[W]hite** Pure white coat. Pink nose leather
[an]d paw pads. Eye colour is vivid blue.
[Bl]ack Dense coal black coat. Black nose
[le]ather. Black or seal brown paw pads.
[Ey]e colour is vivid green.

Blue Blue-grey coat. Blue-grey nose
leather and paw pads. Eye colour is vivid
green.
Chocolate Warm chocolate brown coat.
Milk chocolate nose leather. Paw pads
are cinnamon to milk chocolate. Eye
colour is vivid green.
Lilac Coat is a faded lilac with a pinkish
tinge. Nose leather and paw pads are
lavender-pink or faded lilac. Eye colour
is vivid green.
Cinnamon Warm cinnamon brown coat.
Cinnamon brown nose leather. Paw pads
are cinnamon brown to pink. Eye colour
is vivid green.
Caramel A cool-toned bluish-fawn coat.
Bluish-fawn nose leather and paw pads.

Eye colour is vivid green.
Fawn Warm beige-fawn coat. Pinkish-
fawn nose leather. Paw pads are pink or
pinkish-fawn. Eye colour is vivid green.
Red Self Rich, brilliant red coat. Brick
red or pink nose leather and paw pads.
Eye colour is vivid green.
Cream Pale, pure pastel-cream coat.
Pink nose leather and paw pads. Eye
colour is vivid green.

Tortoiseshell Varieties:

With the introduction of the sex-linked
gene which produced the red and the
cream, litters included female kittens of
various combinations of colours in the
pattern called tortoiseshell.
Black Tortie Coat is black patched or
mingled with red and/or light red. Nose
leather and paw pads are black, brick
red, or pink, or black mottled with brick
red and/or pink.
Blue Tortie Coat is light blue-grey
patched or mingled with pale cream.
Nose leather and paw pads are blue-grey
or pink, or blue-grey with pink.
Chocolate Tortie Coat is milk
chocolate patched or mingled with red
or light red. Nose leather is milk
chocolate, pale red or pink, or milk
chocolate mottled with pale red and/or
pink. Paw pads are cinnamon to milk
chocolate, pale red or pink, or cinnamon
to milk chocolate mottled with pale red
and/or pink.

*This Oriental Blue Tortie
is most striking with his
vivid green eyes and
elegant form.*

Lilac Tortie Coat is a faded lilac with a pinkish tinge, patched or mingled with pale cream. Nose leather and paw pads are lavender-pale pink, or lavender-pink mottled with pale pink.

Cinamon Tortie Coat is a warm cinnamon brown patched with red or light red. Nose leather and paw pads are cinnamon brown, pinkish-red or pink, or cinnamon brown mottled with pinkish-red and/or pink.

Caramel Tortie Coat is a cool-toned bluish-fawn patched or mingled with rich beige and/or cream. Nose leather and paw pads are bluish-fawn or pink or bluish-fawn mottled with pink.

Tabby:
Oriental tabbies may have Classic, Mackerel, Spotted or Ticked tabby patterns. In the Classic, there should be dense and clearly defined broad markings In Mackerel tabbies, there should be clearly defined stripes. For the Spotted, regular, round spots are preferred. In all Oriental tabbies, frown marks on the forehead form a letter M.

Black Tabby Base coat is coppery brown with black markings. Backs of legs are black. Nose leather is black or brick red rimmed with black. Paw pads are black or seal brown. Eye colour is green.

Blue Tabby Base coat is pale bluish-ivory with blue-grey markings. Backs of legs are a darker shade of blue-grey. Nose leather is blue or old rose, rimmed with blue. Paw pads are blue-grey or rose. Eye colour is green.

Chocolate Tabby Base coat is a warm fawn with chocolate brown markings. Backs of legs are chocolate brown. Nose leather is chocolate or pale red rimmed with chocolate. Paw pads are cinnamon to chocolate. Eye colour is green.

Lilac Tabby Base coat is off-white to palest lilac, with rich lilac or lavender markings. Backs of legs are a darker shade of lilac. Nose leather is lavender or pink rimmed with lavender. Paw pads are lavender-pink. Eye colour is green.

Red Tabby Base coat is red with deep red markings. Backs of legs are dark red. Nose leather is brick red or pink. Paw pads are pink (Europe), brick red (USA). Eye colour is copper to green.

Cream Tabby Base coat pale cream with buff or cream markings. Backs of legs are dark cream. Nose leather and paw pads are pink. Eye colour is copper to green.

Cinnamon Tabby Base coat is deep apricot with cinnamon brown markings. Backs of legs are cinnamon brown. Nose leather is pale pink. Paw pads are cinnamon brown to pinkish-brown.

Caramel Tabby Base coat is cool-toned beige with cool-toned bluish-fawn markings. Backs of legs are darker bluish-fawn. Nose leather is bluish-fawn, or pink rimmed with bluish-fawn. Paw pads are pink to bluish-fawn.

Fawn Tabby Base coat is dull beige with beige-brown markings. Backs of legs are darker beige-fawn. Nose leather is pink. Paw pads are pinkish-fawn.

Silver Tabby Base coat is pale silver with dense black markings. Backs of legs are black. Nose leather is black or brick red with black rims. Paw pads are black.

Tortie Tabby Can be of any colour recognized in the Oriental group. Coat patched or mingled with areas of red or light red in the non-dilute colours, rich beige or fawn in the Caramel and Fawn. Nose leather is the solid base colour, pink-rimmed with the base colour, or basic colour mottled with pink. Paw pads are basic colour mottled with pink. Eye colour is copper to green.

Smoke, Shaded and Tipped Varieties:
Once silver had been added to the Oriental breeding programme, it wasn't long before cats with short, fine, silvery-white coats were bred with various amounts of tipping. In the Smoke, the hairs are tipped with the appropriate colour and have a narrow silver-white band at the roots. In the Shaded, the hair is tipped to about one-third of its length. The undercoat is white, producing the characteristic sparkling appearance of this colour group. In the Tipped, the hair is tipped just at the end. The Tipped cat is lighter in overall colour than the Shaded.

The charming Oriental first became popular in the early 1960s when a small number of breeders began mating Siamese cats with British, European and American shorthairs. The aim was to breed a Siamese type, but with a greater variety of colours and patterns. They have been bred to have good stamina, plenty of character and, above all, great beauty.

RUSSIAN BLUE

Origins Legend has it that the Russian Blue is a descendant of ships' cats brought from the White Sea in northern Russia to Britain in the 1800s. The modern Russian Blue contains bloodlines derived in part from British Blues and from Blue Point Siamese, consequences of Swedish and British efforts to revive the breed in the 1950s following its near extinction during World War II. Blue was the original coat colour and is preferred by traditionalists, but black and white coats are also available, especially in Europe and New Zealand.

Appearance The Russian Blue is medium in size with a body that is we muscled but finer-boned than other shorthairs. The legs are long and the ta

262

is of medium length and thickness. The head is wedge-shaped with a nose of medium length and a level chin. The ears are large and pointed with very little hair inside or out. The eyes are large, almond-shaped, widely spaced and vivid green in colour.

Coat The soft, dense, insulating double coat is thick and lustrous, its density causing the coat to stand out from the body. Minimal grooming is required. Some breeders say the coat looks best if it is never brushed.

The Russian Blue is rather a nervous cat, preferring not to be left alone and needing the company of human beings or other pets. They prefer living indoors and make excellent pets for apartment-dwellers.

263

RIGHT, OPPOSITE and
OVERLEAF
*The Russian Blue is said
to be a descendant of
ships' cats brought from
Russia to Britain in the
1800s. The modern
Russian Blue, however,
has elements of the
Siamese and the British
Blue in its bloodline.*

Characteristics and Temperament A
cautious cat, the Russian Blue dislikes
changes in its environment and is shy
with strangers. It needs the company of
humans or other pets. A gentle breed,
the Russian Blue is among the least
destructive of all cats, and considered
by many cat fanciers to be an ideal
indoor companion. It is the perfect
companion for flat-dwellers.

The Russian Blue has a muscular body but is finer-boned than the British and American Shorthairs. It has a thick, dense, double coat, designed to withstand intense cold. The coat is usually blue, but black and white cats are also available. The almond-shaped eyes are a vivid green, contrasting strikingly with the blue coat.

RIGHT, OPPOSITE and OVERLEAF

The Scottish Fold is a placid cat with the habit of tapping its owner with a paw to gain attention. It has been known to fall asleep on it back, with its paws sticking up in the air!

SCOTTISH FOLD

Origins In 1961 a Scottish shepherd noticed a cat with strangely folded ears. This cat, called Susie, was the founder of the breed to which all of today's Scottish Folds are related. A breeding programme was begun in the UK, but it was discovered that the dominant gene that caused the folded ears could also cause skeletal problems. The GCCF, among others, resisted recognition of the breed, and the main centre of activity for the breed switched to the USA. Today's Scottish Fold cats were

developed originally by outcrossings to British Shorthairs and to American Shorthairs in the USA. They now resemble these cats in type, aside from the shape of their ears. Those with normal ears, often described as Scottish Straightears, are mated with cats which have folded ears to avoid genetic problems.

Appearance The Scottish Fold has a round face with wide round eyes and the ears folding tightly forward over the head. The ears should be small with

rounded tips. The body is compact with a short neck. The tail is medium to long, flexible and tapering.

Coat The short, soft, dense coat is kept in good condition with the minimum of brushing and combing. The folded ears should be gently cleaned inside the folds with a damp cotton bud.

Characteristics and Temperament A loving, placid and companionable cat that loves both humans and other pets. These cats can cope with cold, harsh weather and have the farm cat's resistance to disease. Many Scottish Folds have the habit of sitting upright and tapping their owner with a paw. They often sleep on their backs with their legs in the air.

Colours White, Black, Blue, Red, Cream, Tortoiseshell, Calico, Dilute Calico, Blue-cream, Chinchilla, Shaded Silver, Shell Cameo, Black Smoke, Blue Smoke, Cameo Smoke, Bi-colour; Classic and Mackerel Tabby in Brown, Blue, Red, Cream, Cameo, Silver; Patched Tabby in Brown, Blue, Silver. There are both short- and long-coated versions of this breed, differing only in terms of their coat length.

OPPOSITE, LEFT and OVERLEAF
All Scottish Folds are related to one original cat with folded ears that was discovered by a Scottish shepherd in 1961.

The Selkirk Rex is still quite rare, particularly females, as most of them are taking part in breeding programmes. There are males available, however, which make excellent pets.

SELKIRK REX

Origins This naturally curly cat originated from a stray blue-cream and white non-pedigree kitten found in Wyoming, USA in 1987. She was given to a Persian breeder who bred her to a black Persian. She produced three curly kittens out of six, proving that, unlike the Cornish and Devon Rexes (pages 182–191), the mother's mutation was dominant. Because of this, curly kittens can be born in the same litter as straight-haired kittens. Several more breedings proved that she carried the genes for both point restriction and long hair. Because of this, the decision was made

OPPOSITE, LEFT and
OVERLEAF
*The Selkirk Rex is a large
cat with dense bones that
make it feel even heavier
for its size – a reflection
of its Persian ancestry.*

to allow all colours and both hair
lengths in the breed.

Appearance A medium to large cat
with heavy bones that give the cat
surprising weight and an impression of
power, which is a direct reflection of its
Persian ancestry. The head is rounded
with wide cheeks. The eyes are round,
full, and wide-set. Ears are medium and
pointed. The legs are medium and the
paws large. The tail is thick and tapers
to a slightly rounded tip.

Coat The cat has a random,
unstructured coat, arranged in loose,
individual curls. The curls appear in
'clumps' rather than as an overall wave.
Maintaining the curl and coat is the
same as for a longhaired cat, while
combing and brushing before bathing is
necessary. All the hairs are present, but
curled, including the whiskers.

Characteristics and Temperament
These are extremely patient, loving and
tolerant cats with an endearing
personality. There are not many of these
available as pets because most curly
cats, especially females, are in breeding
programmes. Males are usually more
readily available and make wonderful,
affectionate pets. Both longhaired and
shorthaired versions are possible.

OPPOSITE, LEFT AND
OVERLEAF
*The Selkirk Rex breed
began when a curly-
coated female stray was
mated with a black
Persian, when three out
of six of the kittens were
born curly-coated,
proving that the mother's
mutation was dominant.
Several more breedings
proved that she had the
genes for point restriction
as well as long hair.
Therefore, both short and
longhaired types are
possible.*

Siamese have larger-than-life personalities; they are energetic and demanding, so it is better to have at least a pair so that they are kept occupied. They are also very vocal, having a loud voice which is said to resemble a baby crying. Siamese are nevertheless very affectionate and make charming, entertaining companions. They are also elegantly beautiful.

SIAMESE

Origins With its distinctive looks, the Siamese is one of the world's most instantly recognizable breeds. It originated in Asia more than 500 years ago, where it held special status as guardian of the royal temples of Siam (now Thailand), and was revered by monks and royalty alike. In the late 1800s, the first breeding pair were brought to the UK. These were stockier cats with rounder heads than would become the fashion in later years. The popularity of the Siamese peaked around the 1950s. Since then, there has been a decline in their appeal attributed by some to a move towards a more extremely elongated, angular look. Recently, there has been a resurgence of interest in a more traditional 'applehead' look (see Traditional Siamese Cat (page 366).

Appearance These tall and graceful cats have a svelte build, long, slim legs, and a long head. They are also fine-boned with taut muscles. Face-on, the head from the tip of the ears to the muzzle forms a pronounced wedge shape. The eyes are almond-shaped and slanted, and a brilliant clear blue. The ears are very prominent and pointed. The paws are dainty and oval, while the tail is very long, thin at the base and tapering to a fine point.

286

Coat The Siamese has a very short, fine coat that is glossy, silky and close-lying. Grooming is easy but must be done regularly. Young cats are pale at birth and the coloration of their points only emerges gradually.

Characteristics and Temperament An enterprising, lively and playful cat, the Siamese is loyal and affectionate but can be aloof. These cats are famed for their loud voices and big personalities. They make better pets when kept in pairs or small groups. Few cats are more ready to climb, both outdoors and in the home. Once Siamese become sexually mature very early in life – sometimes when just four months old, although six months is more usual – be prepared to arrange for young queens in particular to be neutered at the appropriate stage, to prevent unwanted kittens.

Siamese Varieties

Seal Point Beige to cream or pale fawn body. Dark seal brown points, nose leather and paw pads.

Blue Point Bluish-white body. Blue-grey points, nose leather and paw pads.

Chocolate Point Ivory body. Points are dark chocolate. Milk chocolate nose leather and cinnamon to milk chocolate paw pads.

Siamese cats come in a huge array of colours. On the right is a Chocolate Point, while opposite is a Lilac Point. All Siamese have a rich cream or off-white base coat with coloured points on the ears, mask, tail and legs. They also have brilliant blue eyes.

Lilac Point Glacial white body. Points are frosty grey. Lavender-pink nose leather and paw pads. (This and the three varieties above are considered to be the traditional Siamese colours. Some US registration bodies only accept others as Colourpoint Shorthairs.)

Cinnamon Point Ivory body. Points are warm cinnamon brown. Cinnamon brown or pink nose leather and paw pads.

Caramel Point Off-white body. Points are brownish-grey. Brownish-grey or pink nose leather and paw pads. One of the newer varieties.

Fawn Point Off-white body. Points are a pale rosy mushroom. Mushroom or pink nose leather and paw pads.

Red Point Creamy-white body. Points are a bright, warm orange. Pink nose leather and paw pads.

Cream Point Creamy-white body. Points are a pastel cream. Pink nose leather and paw pads.

Apricot Point Warm creamy-white body. Points are hot cream. Pink nose leather and paw pads.

Seal Tortie Point Beige shading to fawn on body. Points are seal patched with red and/or light red. Seal brown and/or pink nose leather and paw pads.

Blue Tortie Point Bluish-white body. Points are blue-grey patched with

OPPOSITE, LEFT and OVERLEAF
The Siamese is probably the most famous of cat breeds and is the most easily recognizable. They were greatly respected, not only by Siamese royalty but also by Buddhist monks, and descendants of the modern Siamese cat can still be seen wandering the palaces and temples of Bangkok.

shades of pastel cream. Blue-grey or pink nose leather and paw pads.

Chocolate Tortie Point Ivory body. Points are milk chocolate patched with shades of red and/or light red. Milk chocolate and/or pink nose leather and cinnamon to milk chocolate and/or pink paw pads.

Lilac Tortie Point Glacial white body. Points are frosty grey with a pinkish tone patched with pale cream. Pale pink or lavender-pink nose leather and paw pads.

Cinnamon Tortie Point Ivory body. Points are a warm cinnamon brown with shades of red. Cinnamon brown or pink nose leather and paw pads.

Caramel Tortie Point Off-white body. Points are brownish-grey with shades of apricot. Brownish-grey or pink nose leather and paw pads.

Fawn Tortie Point Off-white body. Points are a pale rosy mushroom with shades of cream. Mushroom or pink nose leather and paw pads.

Seal Tabby Point Beige body. Points are dark seal tabby. Brick red, pink or seal brown nose leather. Paw pads are seal brown.

Blue Tabby Point Bluish-white body. Points are blue-grey tabby. Old rose or blue-grey nose leather. Paw pads are blue grey.

Chocolate Tabby Point Ivory body. Points are milk chocolate tabby. Light red, pink

or milk chocolate nose leather. Paw pads are cinnamon to milk chocolate.

Lilac Tabby Point Glacial white body. Points are lilac tabby. Lavender-pink or pink nose leather. Paw pads are lavender-pink.

Red Tabby Point Off-white body with a slight red tinge. Points are a warm orange tabby. Brick red or pink nose leather. Paw pads are pink.

Cream Tabby Point Creamy-white body. Points are cream tabby. Pink nose leather and paw pads.

Cinnamon Tabby Point Ivory body. Points are a warm cinnamon tabby. Cinnamon brown or pink nose leather and paw pads.

Caramel Tabby Point Off-white body. Points are brownish-grey tabby. Brownish-grey or pink nose leather and paw pads.

Fawn Tabby Point Off-white body. Points are a pale rosy mushroom tabby. Mushroom or pink nose leather and paw pads.

Apricot Tabby Point Warm creamy-white body. Points are a hot cream tabby. Pink nose leather and paw pads.

Seal Torbie Point Beige body. Points colour has seal tabby markings mingled with red tortie markings. Seal, brick red or pink nose leather and paw pads. (The description of Torbie is a shorthand favoured especially in North America to

Siamese kittens are much paler than their parents, but as they mature, their point markings become more distinguishable and a richer colour. Opposite, are two Red Point kittens, while left is a little Chocolate Point.

RIGHT
A Blue Point Siamese.

OPPOSITE
Two Lilac Point kittens.

RIGHT, OPPOSITE and
OVERLEAF
*The Siamese is tall and
elegant and has a svelte
body with long, slim legs,
and a triangular-shaped
head. It is also muscular
and athletic.*

...cribe cats which display both ...oiseshell and tabby markings. They ... invariably female, as with other ...e varieties.)

...e Torbie Point Bluish-white body. ...ts colour has blue tabby markings ...gled with cream tortie markings.

Nose leather is blue-grey, old rose or pink. Paw pads are blue-grey and/or pink.

Chocolate Torbie Point Ivory body. Points colour has milk chocolate tabby markings, mingled with red tortie markings. Nose leather is milk chocolate,

pale red or pink. Paw pads are cinnamon to milk chocolate and/or pink.

Lilac Torbie Point Glacial white body. Points colour has lilac tabby markings mingled with cream tortie markings. Nose leather and paw pads are in faded lilac and/or pink.

namon Torbie Point Ivory body.
ts colour has warm cinnamon tabby
kings mingled with red tortie
kings. Cinnamon brown or pink nose
her and paw pads.

Caramel Torbie Point Off-white body.
Points colour has brownish-grey tabby
markings mingled with apricot tortie
markings. Brownish-grey or pink nose
leather and paw pads.

Fawn Torbie Point Off-white body.
Points colour has pale rosy mushroom
tabby markings mingled with cream
tortie markings. Mushroom or pink nose
leather and paw pads.

Singapuras are beautiful, affectionate and gentle. Sadly they are still quite rare and therefore expensive to acquire.

SINGAPURA

Origins During the 1970s, an Americ[an] cat breeder found a colony of unusua[l] looking feral cats in Singapore. They were known as 'drain cats', and at on[e] time were culled by the Singaporeans[.] The cats were first taken to the USA i[n] 1975 and all registered Singapuras to[day] originate from this breeding program[me.] The name 'Singapura' is Malaysian fo[r] Singapore.

During the 1970s, an American noticed some feral cats, which were wandering the streets of Singapore, and was struck by their unusual appearance. Some were taken back to the US where the Singapura breeding programme was soon established.

The Singapura is one of the smallest of cat breeds. It has a ticked tabby coat and startlingly large eyes of either, hazel, green or yellow.

Appearance Ranked as one of the smallest breeds in the world, typicall weighing less than 6lb (2.7kg), the Singapura is nevertheless stocky and muscular in build. Its head is round, ears large and its eyes are huge, almo shaped and coloured brilliant hazel, green or yellow. The nose and eyes a accentuated by dark eye-liner-like outlines. The tail is slightly shorter t the body and slender with a blunt tip

Coat The fine, short, close-lying coat in a ticked tabby with some marking the backs of the legs, but not on the front. Each hair should have at least

RIGHT, OPPOSITE and
OVERLEAF
*The Singapura is
unusual in that it is one
of the few breeds whose
coat comes in only one
form – sepia agouti.*

bands of dark ticking separated by lig
bands of colour. Each individual hair
light next to the skin and dark at the
The Singapura is one of the few breed
that is only available in one colour,
called sepia agouti. It is a warm ivory
overlaid with sepia-brown, with pale
underparts. Grooming is very easy. A
light combing removes dead hairs, an
occasional brushing tones the skin.
Hand-grooming or stroking with a silk
scarf imparts a healthy-looking sheen
the coat.

Characteristics and Temperament T
Singapura is affectionate, good-nature
extremely gentle and playful.
Unfortunately, it is still not widely
available and ranks among the more
costly breeds.

The highly affectionate Snowshoe is a devoted companion and will follow its owner everywhere. In fact, it doesn't enjoy being left alone for long and requires plenty of attention.

SNOWSHOE

Origins The result of a cross between Siamese and American Shorthairs, the Snowshoe originated in the USA in the 1960s. The breed remained little known until the 1980s, since when it has gained in popularity but still remains quite rare. Snowshoes faced opposition from Siamese breeders who feared that its characteristic white feet markings could become widely distributed in Siamese bloodlines if cross-breeding took place; but this fear has proved to be groundless.

Appearance With the distinctive white feet that gave rise to its name, the Snowshoe retains the dark points of the Siamese on its legs, tail, face and ears. Its eye colour is a bright, sparkling blue. The Snowshoe's muscular body is medium to large with medium legs and a medium to large tail. The head is triangular, with large almond-shaped eyes that are slightly slanted and large, pointed ears. As in the case of other large breeds, toms tend to be significantly heavier than queens.

Coat The short to medium, fine, glossy, close-lying coat needs the minimum of grooming with regular gentle brushing.

The Snowshoe is accceptable in any colour of the Siamese Himalyan strain. Below and opposite is a Tabby Point adult and kittens, while right is a Blue Point Snowshoe.

Characteristics and Temperament The Snowshoe is highly gregarious and will follow family members about the house. It hates to be alone and needs a good deal of companionship and attention. Its soft, delicate voice reveals its affectionate nature.

Snowshoe Varieties

The preferred standard recommended for the Snowshoe includes an inverted 'V' between the eyes. The front feet are preferred white only as far as the ankles, while there is a longer gauntlet to the hock on the back legs. As in the case of other cats with pointed markings,

314

Snowshoe kittens are white at birth and develop their coloration slowly over the course of several years. They are accceptable in any colour of the Siames of Himalyan strain.

Seal Point Pale fawn to cream body. Deep seal brown points. Nose leather and paw pads are deep brown or black, pink or a combination of seal and pink.

Blue Point Glacial white body with no cream tinge. Blue-grey points, nose leather and paw pads.

The Snowshow is often referred to as the shorthaired Birman, which is incorrect; the Snowshow is the result of mating a Siamese with an American Shorthair, hence its stocky appearance.

The Sphynx loves the company of human beings and is lively and playful. However, it isn't too keen on other cats.

SPHYNX

Origins The modern Sphynx breeding programme began in 1966 in Toronto, Canada, when an ordinary shorthaired, black-and-white domestic cat gave birth to a hairless male kitten. The breed was developed from mother and son. Subsequently, crosses with Devon rexes have been used to expand the breed's bloodline. The Sphynx is not popular with many cat fanciers, however, and is not widely recognized for show purposes because of health worries resulting from the absence of its coat.

This is a breed essentially suited to indoor living, away from the vagaries of the weather. The lack of fur makes these cats vulnerable to the cold, while exposure to hot sun can lead to sunburn, particularly over largely unpigmented areas of skin.

Appearance The Sphynx is a well built, sturdy cat with a head slightly longer than it is wide, set on a long, slender neck. The large, wide-open ears are tall and the outer edge is in line with the wedge of the face. Cheekbones are

prominent and there are few or no whiskers. It has long, slim legs with elegant rounded paws and long toes. The tail is long and finely tapered. All colours and patterns are acceptable. Colours in the Sphynx are often warmer than they are in cats with coats, because the natural pink of the skin is able to show through.

Coat The suede-like, wrinkled skin is covered with a soft, warm down, like the skin of a peach. There may be visible fur on the brow, around the toes

RIGHT, OPPOSITE and OVERLEAF
The Sphynx is not an outdoor cat; its lack of fur means it can easily get cold and its delicate skin means it is more likely to become sunburned.

and at the tip of the tail. The skin needs daily cleaning, as the cat's empty hair follicles have oil-producing glands that cause it to sweat. People normally allergic to cats may find they can tolerate the furless Sphynx.

Characteristics and Temperament A lively, playful and mischievous cat, the Sphynx is very people-oriented, but does not like being held or petted. They are not keen on other cats.

320

The Tonkinese has inherited all its lively intelligence and curiosity from its Oriental breeding. However, it is less demanding and vocal than the Siamese and makes an excellent pet.

TONKINESE

Origins The Tonkinese displays the physical features of its mixed parentage – the product of a mating between a Siamese and a Burmese in the USA in the 1950s. The Tonkinese has the points of the Siamese, but with a softer-lined body, less angular head and quieter nature. Such mixed parentage means that the matings of two Tonkinese will not produce an all-Tonkinese litter. The result is most likely to be two Tonkinese to one each of Siamese and Burmese.

Appearance The Tonkinese is of medium build, with a wedge-shaped head with high cheekbones and strong

contours to the brow, cheek and profile. The chin is firm and the eys almond-shaped and slanted. The eye colour is blue-green or turquoise. The ears have oval tips and the hair on them is very short. The legs are slim and the paws oval. The tail is medium to long and tapers.

Coat The coat is short, close-lying, fine and soft, with a lustrous sheen. The pattern shades to a darker tone on the legs, ears, mask and tail. The coat colour is paler than the Burmese but darker than the Siamese. It is easy to keep in good condition with very little grooming.

Characteristics and Temperament The Tonkinese has all the lively curiosity and affection of an Oriental breed, but without the loud insistent personality. It is a good choice for a person new to cats and is also suitable for families with children. It is an easy cat to train. Tonkinese cats love the outdoor life and should not be confined to a small flat or left alone for hours on end.

Typical Varieties The mask, ears, legs, paws and tail are densely marked, but gradually merge into the body colour. The colour of the points is the same as the body colour but denser and darker: there is a distinct contrast between the points and body colour whatever the variety.

The Tonkinese is the result of a mating between a Siamese and a Burmese. It is interesting, therefore, that the mother will never have a full litter of Tonkinese; the litter will consist of two Tonks to one each of Siamese and Burmese.

Brown The medium-brown coat shades to a lighter tone on the underparts. Points and nose leather are dark brown. Paw pads are medium to dark brown.

Chocolate The buff-cream body has medium-brown points. Nose leather is cinnamon brown. Paw pads are cinnamon pink to cinnamon brown.

Blue The soft grey-blue coat shades to a lighter tone on the underparts. Points are slate blue (distinctly darker than the body colour). Nose leather and paw pads are blue-grey.

Red The golden-cream coat shades to apricot on the underparts. Points are a light to medium ruddy brown. Nose leather and paw pads are caramel pink.

Lilac The pale silvery-grey coat has warm overtones (not white or cream). Points are pewter grey. Nose leather is lavender-pink or lavender-grey. Paw pads are lavender-pink.

New Varieties
Members of the Cat Association of Britain, working with new colours in Burmese and Siamese cats, decided to introduce these into the Tonkinese. Special awards for Tonkinese are offered in the following colour varieties: seal, blue, chocolate, cinnamon, lilac, fawn, caramel, beige, red, cream, apricot, indigo and all these colours as tortoiseshell, tabby forms.

OPPOSITE, LEFT and OVERLEAF
The Tonkinese, being a mix of the Burmese and Siamese breeds, is not as heavy as the Burmese but not as slight as the Siamese. It appears to have selected the most favourable aspects of both breeds to make it a well balanced and very attractive cat.

NON-PEDIGREE CATS

RIGHT
The non-pedigree cat is no less appealing than the pedigree. In fact, many people prefer moggies as they are more robust and live to be a good age. They may not have the dramatic looks of some of the pedigrees, but make equally attractive and loving companions.

OPPOSITE
This little tabby is going through all the motions of stalking prey, behaviour which is instinctual and in her genetic make-up.

Origins Of the 100 million or more pet cats worldwide, non-pedigrees (or random-bred or 'moggies', if you prefer) vastly outnumber pedigree cats. Up until the end of the 1800s, people mostly kept cats in order to keep down the vermin in their houses and barns. Only the rich kept cats for fun. It was with the introduction of specific breeding programmes that the concept of the pedigree (and therefore non-pedigree) cat was born. While some people favour the looks, character traits and habits of pedigree cats, a happy, healthy moggie can be every bit as rewarding. Due to the endless possible combinations in their ancestry, a moggie's appearance and character is, of course, unpredictable. However, a great many people feel it's worth taking the risk for the sake of a friendly companion.

Appearance Some non-pedigree cats closely resemble particular breeds. However, most have the moderate build that is typical of the British and American Shorthairs. Apart from colour and coat, moggies differ much less from each other than pure breeds do, having not acquired the extremes of cobbiness or elongation that have been introduced into pedigree lines by selective breeding. Wedge-shaped heads and flattened faces are unusual in moggies but do sometimes appear if one of the parents includes a cat with Siamese or Persian genes in its

recent history. Eyes are usually green or yellow and most non-pedigree cats have fairly long noses.

Coat Because the gene determining short hair is dominant, most cross-bred cats are shorthaired, but there is no standard cross-bred type.

Characteristics and Temperament In general, non-pedigree cats are energetic, as this is nature's way of selecting the fittest and most successful animals. A distinct advantage of owning a moggie is that they have much lower concentrations of undesirable genes and are therefore less prone to disability and disease. With proper care, a non-pedigree cat should live a long life. The typical moggie, if you choose carefully, is a beautiful, intelligent, playful, low-maintenance companion with an independent streak.

Typical Colours Many moggie cats are tabbies, which is the variety closest to the cat's ancestor – the African wildcat, while bi-colours and tortoiseshells are also common. Solid colours are less common; however, black, white, marmalade and blue do occur, usually broken with traces of white fur, typically under the chin. White is common in moggies, both on its own and in combination with other solid and tabby colours.

OPPOSITE
These non-pedigree kittens are just as appealing as their pedigree cousins; however, it is difficult at this stage to say how they will look when they grow up or what their temperament will be.

LEFT
This older cat is happily passing the hours asleep in his favourite place. Even though he cost next to nothing to acquire, his owner values him as highly as any pedigree cat.

NEWER BREEDS

CALIFORNIA SPANGLED

Origins The California Spangled cat resulted from the deliberate effort of Paul Casey, an American screenwriter who, on a trip to Africa, became horrified by the destruction of the wild African cats. He decided to breed a domestic cat that looked something like the leopards and other wild felines, but with a gentle nature. The programme started in 1971, using non-pedigree cats from Asia and Egypt, and a range of pedigree cats including Abyssinian, Siamese and Manx. By 1991, the breed had been accepted by two American associations (TICA and the ACA). The introduction of the cat to the public was quite unusual: in 1986 Spangled kittens appeared in a well-known Christmas mail-order catalogue, in 'any color clients may desire to match their clothes or their house decorations' – as 'designer' cats. The California Spangled was an instant hit, and Casey used the publicity to launch a new effort to stop the destruction of wild cats in Central and South America.

Appearance Long, low, well-muscled body. The head is medium-sized and rounded with prominent cheekbones and powerful jaws. It has almond-shaped eyes and round-tipped ears.

OPPOSITE and LEFT
The California Spangled cat was bred to resemble the wild cats whose numbers are continuing to decrease alarmingly. Its claim to fame is that it is the most expensive cat in the world.

RIGHT, OPPOSITE and OVERLEAF
The distinctive California Spangled cat has a dense coat with spotted and striped markings; but for its size, wouldn't look out of place roaming the plains of Africa. Because of its value, however, it is better kept as a house cat.

paws are long and strong. The tail is medium to long, with a black tip.

Coat The short, plush, dense double coat is marked with distinctive round black spots, and stripes between the ears and down the neck to the shoulders. Weekly brushing is all that is required.

Characteristics and Temperament
Good-tempered and unusually intelligent, the California Spangled is a lively and extremely active cat.

Typical Colours Black; Blue; Bronze; Brown; Charcoal; Gold; Red; Silver; White.

RIGHT, OPPOSITE and
OVERLEAF
*The Munchkin has been
bred to have short legs,
making it the Dachshund
of the feline world. It has
only been recognized as
a breed since 1995,
however, and is still very
rare.*

MUNCHKIN

Origin The Munchkin originated as a
spontaneous genetic mutation in
Louisiana, USA, in 1983. This resulted
in a cat with disproportionately short
legs that have caused it to be the subject
of considerable controversy. The
Munchkin cat was recognized as a new
breed by TICA in 1995. Although the
Munchkin is new to breed associations,
cats with short legs were known in
Europe during the first part of the 20th
century, but seem to have died out. Now,
demand for Munchkins far exceeds the
supply, and they are gradually becoming
more numerous in Europe as well as
North America.

Appearance The body and head are
medium-sized, the ears quite large and
triangular, and the eyes large and
walnut-shaped. The legs are
significantly shorter than those of other
cats, but straight with slightly turned-out
paws. The tail is of medium thickness,
tapering to a rounded tip.

Coat Both longhaired and shorthaired
varieties are available.

Characteristics and Temperament
Despite the short legs, Munchkins can
run extremely fast. They are able to

RIGHT, OPPOSITE and OVERLEAF
Munchkins tend to have bi-coloured or tabby coats, though other coats are possible, and despite their short legs are agile and perfectly capable of climbing trees.

climb trees as well as any other cat; however, they do not jump as high because the shorter back legs do not give the same degree of leverage. Munchkins are playful, outgoing and love to be handled. They are very sociable and intelligent, and enjoy company. Friendly and self-assured, the Munchkin gets on well with other pets, too.

Typical Colours The Munchkin comes in a variety of colours and patterns. Tabbies and Bi-colours are more common than Oriental shades and patterns.

The beautiful Nebelung has the same colouring as the Russian Blue, except that the luxurious coat is long and tipped with silver, giving it an almost iridescent effect. They also come in white, though the blue is most common.

NEBELUNG

Origins The Nebelung – whose name means 'mist-creature' in German – is a new, longhaired version of the Russian Blue that was developed in the USA in the 1980s. In 1987, the breed was accepted by TICA and it was also recognized by the TCA in 1990; but other major registries have not accepted it. Although the Nebelung is gaining popularity, it is still not very well known.

Appearance Similar in all respects to the Russian Blue except for the coat length, the Nebelung is a rather delicate-looking cat, with a long body, legs and tail, and green eyes.

Coat The double coat is long, fine and soft. The guard hairs are silver-tipped. Daily grooming is required.

Characteristics and Temperament
The Nebelung is calm, gentle and can be playful. Although the Nebelung is loving and affectionate, it may not be the best choice for a family with small children, because it is timid and has a reserved personality.

Typical Colours Blue is most common, although there is also a white variety.

The Ojos Azules is very rare, its Spanish name meaning 'blue eyes'; indeed, its eyes are of such as intense blue that they outshine those of the Siamese.

OJOS AZULES

Origins One of the rarest breeds, the Ojos Azules (which means 'Blue Eyes' in Spanish) has evolved mainly in New Mexico, USA, since the 1980s. Unlike other blue-eyed cats, the dominant gene that causes the Ojos Azules' blue eyes is not linked to deafness. The breed remains rare because of the possibilty that the mutation that causes the blue eyes may also be linked to a lethal gene. For this reason, too, the breed is not widely recognized. In 1992 only ten cats had been registered.

Appearance Triangular head, medium body, hind legs slightly longer than fore legs. Small paws. Eyes are large and round and a brilliant dark blue.

Coat This breed can occur in both long and shorthaired variations and needs only regular brushing to maintain the coat.

Characteristics and Temperament Active, friendly and affectionate.

Typical Colours The Ojos Azules is acceptable in many colours (white is typically not encouraged) and is commonly seen in the tortoiseshell pattern. The wide number of colours common to the Ojos Azules is highly unusual since most blue-eyed cats are either white, or pointed (such as the Siamese).

The Pixiebob bears a striking resemblance to the wild American bobcat, and despite its supposedly wild heritage is kind and affectionate.

PIXIEBOB

Origins The Pixiebob bears a striking resemblance to the wild North American bobcat, and may indeed be a result of a mating of a wild cat and a farm cat. Originally developed in Washington State, USA, in the 1990s, the founding cat, Pixie, gave her name to the breed. Polydactyl (many-toed) paws are a common occurrence in the breed, but do not hinder the ability of these cats to get around. The breed was accepted by TICA in 1998.

Appearance The cat is muscular and heavy-boned, of a medium to large size, with large feet and a bobbed tail. The head is a medium to large pear-shape with slightly rounded ears. The eyes are medium and deep-set. A straight-footed Pixiebob has the normal number of toes: five at the front, and four at the back. The polydactyl Pixiebob has seven toes on each of the front feet.

Coat The coat can be short or semi-long, with patterns of spots and rosettes, and requires minimum grooming.

Characteristics and Temperament
Despite its possibly wild heritage, the Pixiebob is truly domesticated. Loyal, trustworthy, gentle, affectionate, Pixiebobs thrive on attention. They do not readily change homes and prefer to be the sole pet.

Pixiebob kittens.

The Ragamuffin is related to the Ragdoll but, unlike it, comes in a variety of colours and points.

RAGAMUFFIN

Origins Ragamuffins are closely associated with their ancestors, the Ragdolls. They were bred specifically for their sweet temperament and were designated as a separate breed in 1994. Ragdolls are recognized for competition only in limited colours, but the Ragamuffin is available in many colours, including all pointed colour varieties.

Appearance The head is a medium-sized, broad, modified wedge. The nose is medium and the eyes are large, oval, expressive and inquisitive. Ears are medium-sized, with a slight forward tilt and rounded tips. The very large body is heavy, firm and muscular with a full chest. The tail is long and fluffy with a slight taper and carried higher than the back.

Coat The coat is luxuriantly long or semi-long, plush and silky and shorter on the face. The coat length varies slightly, but in general it is low-maintenance compared to that of other longhaired breeds.

Characteristics and Temperament Ragamuffins make ideal pets for the first-time cat owner. They are one of the most relaxed, perfectly happy cats you are ever likely to encounter, with an

The Ragamuffin has an extremely docile and loving nature. It is best kept as an indoor pet, however, as its trusting nature and extreme docility can easily lead it to danger.

unusually docile and warm disposition. They are true people-loving cats and get along well with children and other pets, and they love to be where the action is. They also tend to be soft-pawed (they rarely put out their claws). The Ragamuffin is suitable only as an indoor pet. They don't possess the defence instincts of most other cats, so they need protection.

Typical Colours All varieties of point colours: red, tortie, mink, sepia, seal, blue, chocolate or lilac; all mink and sepia colours; all colours of Persians in solids, mitted, and parti-colours. There are many colours/patterns available, including Selfs, Tabbies, Torties, and Blue-eyed pointed varieties.

The Savannah is the result of breeding from a serval and a domestic Bengal cat. The result is a cat which still retains something of its wild heritage with quiet domestic traits superimposed. In fact, it seems to have the best of both worlds as well as being extremely beautiful.

SAVANNAH

Origins The Savannah is named after
African grasslands where its close
relative, the serval cat, is to be found,
which also helped to lay the
foundations for the breed: the first and
subsequent generations derived from the
breeding of a serval to a domestic
Bengal cat. The International
Progressive Cat Breeders' Alliance
(IPCBA) was the first international all-
breed registry to recognize Savannahs
for registration. The goal of the
Savannah breeding programme was to
create a domestic cat which has
physical features that link it with the
serval, but combined with the loving,
dependable temperament of the typical
domestic cat.

Appearance The Savannah has a large,
muscular build, a long neck and large,
round ears, with distinctive black 'tear
drop' markings on the eyes.

Savannah kittens.

Characteristics and Temperament
The Savannah has a reasonably docile temperament. They make great family pets and are easy to care for. They are loyal, intelligent and have an outgoing personality. They make excellent companions for children as well as other pets.

Coat The sleek coat is spotted, striped or marbled.

Typical Colours Amber, Silver, Solid Black, Black Smoke.

The modern Siamese has been bred to look sleek and lean, a far cry from the original traditional Siamese, pictured here, which is stockier and with a more rounded head. It also has a quieter temperament than today's Siamese.

TRADITIONAL SIAMESE (APPLEHEAD)

Origins Traditional Siamese (also known as Appleheads due to their head-shape) are the original cats of the royal family of Siam (now Thailand). These cats were used to guard the temples probably as far back as the 14th century. Appleheads were introduced into Europe towards the end of the 19th century. In recent years, the standard in cat shows for the Siamese breed is to have a stylized, very elongated wedge-shaped head – far removed from the more rounded head of the original Siamese. The Applehead is no longer acknowledged as being Siamese and, therefore, not professionally shown, apart from at traditional cat shows. CFA-Registered Traditional Siamese have become extremely rare. Currently, the Applehead is enjoying something of a revival as cat owners favour a return to the traditional, round-headed look. This has, in part, been driven by fears of health problems ensuing from the very exaggerated, elongated head-shape that found favour in the 1950s.

Appearance A round face and muscular body. Distinctive blue eyes.

Characteristics and Temperament
The temperament is relatively calm and

The traditional Siamese is elegant and graceful, though like its modern counterpart it is demanding and very vocal; but it is also loyal and loving. These are healthy cats and are usually long-lived.

generally considered to be less frenetic than the modern Siamese. Applehead cats are agile, demonstrative, graceful, loyal, affectionate, devoted, intelligent and resourceful. However, they can be domineering, and they are very vocal.

Colours Blue, Chocolate, Lilac and Seal point colours.

The Sokoke Forest Cat originated in East Africa. It is slender and athletic, with vivid green eyes. The coat is very short with agouti tabby-like markings.

SOKOKE FOREST CAT

Origins The original home of the Sokoke Forest Cat was amid the rain forests of East Africa, on the Kenyan coast in the Sokoke Arabuke Forest. Little was known about the Sokoke cat until 1978, when a Kenyan farmer four an unusual litter of kittens on her plantation. A breeding pair was taken Denmark around 1980, where a litter was born in 1985. The breed is still under development in Europe, mainly Denmark where stock was imported directly from the breed's African homeland. The Sokoke was recognize by FIFe in 1993.

Appearance Modified wedge-shaped head, tufted ears, almond-shaped amb to light-green eyes. The Sokoke's slender, muscular, strongly-boned, medium-long body has long back legs that are longer than the fore legs. The tail is long, thin and whip-like.

Coat The coat is extremely short and shiny (not silky), with little or no undercoat.

Colour Agouti hairs appear in the s areas, giving a modified classic tabby pattern. The colour varies from a wa light brown to an almost black chest brown. Tail tip is always black.

Characteristics and Temperament
Almost dog-like in its nature, the
Sokoke is loving and develops a strong
bond with its owner; but it is not the
clinging type. Highly intelligent,
Sokokes enjoy the company of human
beings and in fact 'join in', since they
are eloquent 'talkers' that use a high-
level voice as well as body language.
Both curious and sweet, Sokokes are
very sensitive cats that tend to reflect
the moods of human company. They
thrive in groups, get along well with
other cats, and are a practical size for a
family pet.

Breeds in Development

OPPOSITE

The Poodle Cat is a cross between the curly-coated Devon Rex and a Scottish Fold Cat. It has a most unusual appearance and is possibly not to everyone's liking.

Breeders are still seeking to develop new breeds, not all of which have become popular. None of the breeds mentioned below have reached international recognition status as yet, but in all cases this is vital to safeguard the survival of the breeds. Without it, breeders have little incentive to continue to breed these obscure cats if they have no hope of exhibiting them in due course.

Chausie

A new breed that combines the exoticism of a wild jungle cat with the temperament and eating habits of a domestic cat. The breed was registered with TICA in 1995. The Chausie's silky coat comes in many colours, including golden, black, silver-tipped and leopard-spotted. Chausies are large. They have a long body type, and their hind legs rise slightly higher than the front. They are extremely intelligent and highly active, their muscular build and wild ancestry enabling them to be most athletic. Chausies get on well with other cats.

Highland Lynx

This cat was developed by crossing two existing breeds, the Desert Lynx (a bobcat hybrid) and the Jungle Curl. The Highland Lynx has the body of the bobcat with the distinctive curled ears of the Jungle Curl. These cats are inquisitive and want to be a part of household activities. They come in both long and shorthaired varieties as well as in tawny, leopard and marble patterning. Many Highland Lynx are polydactyl (typically six-toed in this case).

Honeybear

A breeder in California, USA, created the Honeybear by crossing a male that was said to have selected skunk genes injected into it, with Persian females. These large and extremely affectionate felines have very friendly dispositions, despite supposedly having a bit of the skunk in their heritage! Honeybears love children and also get on well with other family pets. Daily brushing is all that is needed to keep the coat looking its best.

Desert Lynx

The Desert Lynx is the result of pairing a wild bobcat with a domestic cat, but bred to resemble their wild cousins as closely as possible, with ear tufts, ruff, coat pattern and size very much like the wild bobcat. They have slightly slanted, almond-shaped eyes and often have polydactyl toes with toe tufts. In contrast with its feral looks, the Desert Lynx has the docile nature of a moggie, and is selectively bred to maintain and continually improve this gentle disposition. Desert Lynx cats can have either a short or longer coat, and have very large, muscular bodies with powerful hindquarters. They are very intelligent and although they can be wary with strangers, they are affectionate towards their owners.

Poodle Cat

A cat that pairs the Devon Rex's curly hair with the folded ears of the Scottish Fold. The Poodle Cat is medium-sized, muscular and surprisingly heavy. Its eyes are large and round, and while copper is the preferred colour, all variations are allowed, provided they match the coat colour. The Poodle Cat has a well proportioned, slightly heart-shaped head. The ears are folded and widely-set, and tend to be larger than the ears of its Scottish Fold ancestor. The legs are of medium length, ending in round paws. The tail is also of medium length. The Poodle Cat's coat lies in dense, silky curls in a variety of colours and patterns. It is a relatively new breed that originated in Germany the 1980s or 90s. As with the Scottish Fold, Poodle Cats should only be mated with cats with straight ears, to avoid risk of crippling skeletal problems in offspring.

RIGHT and OPPOSITE
Poodle Cats.

CAT CARE

RIGHT and OPPOSITE
*Whatever you choose, an
adult cat or a kitten, first
make sure that it is
healthy. This handsome
adult cat looks in the
peak of condition and
the kittens are lively and
alert, always a sign of
good health.*

BRINGING YOUR CAT HOME

Once you have pondered the pleasures
and pitfalls of owning a cat and
decided to go ahead, it is vital to consider
a thorough health check. The cat's coat
should be silky and clean and free from
parasites. The stomach should he soft
with no lumps which could indicate the
presence of roundworms. The ears should
be clean and free from excessive discharge
and parasites and the eyes, mouth and
nose appear healthy, while the anal area
should be clean and unsoiled. Should any
adverse signs be detected at this stage, it
would be wise to withdraw from the
transaction; the cat could have any one of
a number of life-threatening diseases
which could prove expensive to treat and
traumatic for you should the cat die or
have to be destroyed.

Before removing a cat from the care of
its previous owner, it is wise to ask as
many questions as possible relating to its
health, likes and dislikes. This makes life
easier for you once you get the cat home,
as rejected food and toys can be expensive
mistakes. Make sure you also take away
any vaccination records and pedigree
certificates. In this way you can keep tabs
on your cat's medical history and
parentage. If any inoculations have lapsed
or are due, get your vet to do them
straight away; this is not only life-
threatening, it will also prevent you from

Make sure you have all your equipment to hand before bringing your new pet home. This way, the animal will settle into a routine with the minimum of fuss.

boarding your cat in a cattery if you suddenly have to be away from home. Proprietors of catteries check very carefully that all inoculations are up to date; the last thing they want is diseases spreading to their other charges.

Choose the time of collection carefully as it is wise to be at home all day, every day, for the first few days to allow your cat to completely adjust to his new surroundings.

Make sure all necessary equipment and toys are purchased prior to arrival so that everything is to hand to allow the new arrival to settle in as quickly as possible.

ESSENTIAL ITEMS

Cat Carriers There are many different types of these available, constructed from plastic, wicker, or coated wire. They also vary in size, so make sure you select the correct one for your cat and remember that if it is young, it is likely to grow; allow for this fact when making your choice as it will be used throughout your cat's life for trips to the vet or cattery, or even when you move to another home, so it is best to choose one that is sturdily made, of good quality, and big enough.

Beds There are many types available and provided they are of adequate size and strength, most will be suitable. The

traditional wicker bed and blanket or the beanbag are both popular choices. Beds with removable, washable cushions are particularly suitable, as regular washing helps prevent the spread of parasites and keeps them smelling fresh. To cut costs, most cats will be perfectly happy in a cardboard box with the front cut away. Old clothes or blankets can he added for warmth and comfort. Probably the most luxurious bed of all is the sheepskin hammock which fixes over the top of a radiator. During the winter, when the radiator is switched on, your cat will greatly appreciate this additional warm and luxury.

...ed Bowls Purpose-made bowls come ...many sizes but it is not strictly ...cessary to buy them; old kitchen ...ects will do just as well. However, ...ke sure animals' bowls are easily ...ntifiable: it is not a good idea to mix ...m with utensils used by human ...ngs for reasons of hygiene, and they ...uld always be washed and dried ...arately. Cats' bowls should also be ...shed each time they are used. Make ...e fresh water is available at all times.

...er Trays Again, these come in a ...ety of shapes and sizes and some ...n have clip-on lids to prevent litter ...bad smells from escaping.

Depending on your budget, it is preferable to get the best you can afford as the smaller, flimsier trays allow litter to escape over the sides and the plastic is easily cracked. Buy a tray that is on the large side with reasonably high sides which will take a good deep layer of litter; this is more economical in the long run. Soiled clumps should be regularly removed and the litter topped up, the whole lot being replaced at the end of each week. If you try to be too economical by using just a thin layer of litter, you will end up having to remove the whole lot every day.

If your cat is to be eventually allowed outside, the litter tray can be stored away and only brought into use at such times that you wish to restrict your cat to the home, e.g. when he is injured or sick.

For a cat which is to be kept permanently indoors, the litter tray will become a feature of its existence and it is best to find a convenient place for it away from areas where people gather for meals or tend to congregate. The scoop is a vital tool which will enable you to clean out the tray without getting your hands soiled. However, even if your hands do not touch the tray or litter, you should still wash them thoroughly afterwards.

There are many different kinds of

WHAT TO LOOK FOR IN A HEALTHY KITTEN

Nose Should be clean with no discharge, or sneezing.

Mouth Breath should be pleasant-smelling, the teeth straight and white, and the gums pink.

Coat Should be clean and shiny, with no bald itchy patches. Check for evidence of fleas.

Body Should be symmetrical and well grown. Body movements should be agile and supple.

Ears Should be clean and pink inside, free from discharge or redness and with no unpleasant odour.

Eyes Should be clear and bright, and the under-lids should be a healthy pink. There should be no redness or watering.

Anus Should be free from swelling or irritation as well as clean and dry.

Skin Should be clean and free from dandruff, blemishes and sore patches.

Limbs There should be no evidence of lameness. The kitten should be able to stand squarely and should be active and fluid in all his movements.

Expensive bedding isn't really necessary; this little kitten is just as happy snuggled up in an old blanket.

litter, ranging from compressed pellets to fuller's earth and you will soon find one which meets your cat's needs. Some prefer certain types and certain cats will reject litter which has a deodorant in it.

Grooming Tools It is a good idea to get your cat accustomed to being groomed from the very start. All cats need grooming, so purchase tools suitable for its coat length and type.

Collars A collar bearing a tag with you name and address on it is one of the be ways of identifying a lost cat or one which has been involved in an acciden The collar must be either quick-release or elasticated to allow it to come off easily should it become caught on a branch or other object.

Cat Flaps There are many types of these, but it is wise to choose a sturdy one as they take a good deal of punishment once your cat has become accustomed to coming and going. It is surprising how quickly cats learn to u them and once installed they will certainly make life easier for both cat and owner who no longer has to open and close doors each time the cat wis to go in or out. In neighbourhoods wh there are many cats around, it can become a problem when next door's

FAR LEFT
Cats are naturally clean animals and kittens quickly learn how to use a litter tray. Make sure that it is cleaned out regularly.

LEFT
If you allow your cat outside, a cat flap is the ideal solution, as it can come and go as it pleases.

decides to come through your cat flap and into your home. If unwanted guests are a problem, you could choose a flap which can only be activated to open by a small magnet attached to your own cat's collar and will therefore not operate if other cats attempt to enter.

Toys Cats love to play and it is a good idea to get them accustomed to playing with their own toys. Small balls, string, or more elaborate manufactured toys can provide many hours of fun for both cat and owner.

Scratching Posts Cats need to try out their claws and mark out their territory

LEFT
Longhaired cats require daily grooming to keep their fine coats free from tangles. Shorthaired cats need less attention, but it is still wise to groom them, when they can be checked for general health and that there are no adverse skin conditions present.

When your kitten is old enough, you may decide to let him go outside. Although there are dangers lurking, this is a more natural environment for him, and he will be happier as a result.

and when allowed outside will use trees for the purpose. However, should he decide that the house is a place for scratching and that your sofa, stair carpet or curtains are the targets, it may be wise to get a scratching post, especially if he i an indoor cat with no access to a yard or garden when it becomes an essential iter

The arrival of a new cat or kitten is a exciting time when you can at last spend time together, although a new environment will be enough to unnerve the most confident of characters. Make sure that you have transported your cat using some bedding taken from your ow home which will accustom him to the unique smell of your house prior to his arrival.

At first, it is advisable to refrain fro using vacuum cleaners, washing machines and other noisy appliances s as not to alarm him. Once he is confident in his surroundings, you ca begin to use them again.

Before releasing the cat from his carrier, ensure all doors and windows are closed to prevent a nervous cat fro bolting and it is a good idea to restric him to one room only at first. Once h has thoroughly settled, other rooms c be opened up to him which he can th explore at his leisure.

Allow your cat to wander out of l carrier, letting him sniff your hands

Kittens love to play, either with an elaborate toy like this or a ball of string, which he will find equally entertaining.

before touching him and try not to make
sudden movements. As his confidence
grows it is important to reassure him by
stroking him and talking to him gently
and in a low voice. It may be his first
experience away from his mother and it
is therefore up to you to make him feel
secure.

Shortly after his arrival, show him
his food and water bowls, his litter tray
and bed. Make sure you continue to feed
the type of food he was accustomed to at
his previous home. This way you will
avoid possible stomach upsets during his
first days with you.

It is important that his bed is warm
and secluded and provided with plenty
of bedding; at this stage, keep his water
bowl, food and litter tray close by.

From the very beginning, it is wise to
establish certain rules, as cats seem to
prefer a routine. If certain rooms in the
house are to be out of bounds or you
decide never to allow your cat onto your
bed, establish this from the very start,
keeping doors to forbidden areas firmly
closed. If your cat has never been
allowed to enter certain rooms, it is
unlikely that he will persist in the
future.

Should you decide to allow him
roam freely outside, it is important t
you keep him restricted to your hom
at least two weeks to allow him to
establish his territory and gain
confidence. It is a nerve-racking
experience the first time you let him
and it is advisable that you accompa
him and keep an eye on him the firs
times he goes out alone. Cat or kitte
both must be fully vaccinated before
being allowed out at all.

If the cat is to be perpetually
confined to the house, make sure th
never gets a taste of freedom, or he w
be forever trying to escape and may
become listless and unhappy as a res

RIGHT

Contrary to popular opinion, cats and dogs can get on very well together, particularly if both or one of them is a kitten or puppy. Remember to make introductions gradually and don't leave new acquaintances alone until you are confident that they are perfectly safe together.

OPPOSITE

In some cases, however, other pets are nothing more than a tasty meal for a cat. So keep fish and pet rodents out of harm's way.

HANDLING YOUR CAT

The way you pick up a cat is most important, as doing this roughly or incorrectly could be injurious. Don't be tempted to pick him up by the scruff of his neck as a mother cat would her kitten. Pick him up by placing one hand under the chest just behind the front legs. Next, place your other hand under the rump to support his weight, before lifting him up into the crook of your arm.

Meeting Other Pets

This can be tricky, but providing you are patient, things should work out well in the end. It is easier to introduce a kitten than an adult as a kitten poses less of a threat to an animal which is already in residence and immediately assumes a lower place in terms of the pecking order. As a kitten, it is more likely to accept a new situation and will often adopt passive postures, such as rolling onto its back to avoid a confrontation. The older resident animal will be understandably jealous of the new arrival, so expect a certain amount of hissing and spitting at first. Make sure you stroke both animals in turn, transferring their scents one to the other. Cats have a good sense of smell and this will serve to bond them together. At this time, make sure you give an older,

RIGHT
When holding a cat, support its entire body. Never pick a cat up by its limbs or by the scruff of its neck as you could inflict severe damage.

OPPOSITE
Provided that you teach your children the correct way to handle cats and to respect animals in general, there is no reason why they should not become firm friends.

jealous cat slightly more attention. In this way he will be reassured that he is not being completely supplanted. Make sure you do not leave the animals alone together until you are completely satisfied that they have accepted one another and are now firm friends. The same procedure applies to introducing an adult cat, but be slightly more cautious that an aggressive situation does not develop which could eventually lead to a fight.

When a new cat meets the resident dog, special care should be taken as dog can inflict great harm or death on a kitten and an adult cat could converse injure a dog. Keeping the dog adequate restrained, allow the two to introduce themselves to one another gradually, repeating the process over a few days. Stroke both pets to transfer scents fron one to the other. Allowing them to fee from their bowls while together in the same room will help consolidate the relationship. Whatever animal you are attempting to introduce to the other, not leave them unattended until you completely sure that it is absolutely s to do so.

Cats and Children
Cats have always played an importan part in family life and the birth of a baby should not make parents feel th

heir cat is now redundant. However, here are sensible precautions you should take to ensure both baby and cat can co-exist safely in the same house.

Prior to the birth of the baby, ensure that you keep the nursery out of bounds, keeping the cat firmly excluded from the room. Should he sneak in when the door ajar, tell him firmly NO and repeat the process until he begins to get the idea. In the weeks leading up to the birth, reduce the amount of time you spend playing with and petting your cat, as once the baby arrives your attention will be demanded elsewhere, and it is wise to accustom the cat to expect less of it early enough. After the birth, try not to exclude your cat completely. Make sure you give him all the attention you can when time permits.

A cat will never intentionally harm a baby; however, they should not be left alone together. Babies in prams or cots, surrounded by warm bedding, are liable to attract a passing cat who may decide to curl up for a nap on or near the baby's head. Therefore, make sure you use a cat net cover, pulling it tightly over the cot to deter the curious cat.

In all households where pets live, not only when a new baby is involved, hygiene should be paramount. Be sure you wash your hands after handling any animal and keep their toys

and equipment well away from babies and young children.

Provided that a set of ground rules is observed, there is no reason why children and cats cannot mix successfully. From an early age, children must be taught the correct way of approaching and handling them and to treat them with the respect they deserve. It must be made quite clear that a cat is not a toy, but a living creature which should be treated as such. Children bond well with animals and the interaction between pet and child will enrich the lives of them both. A cat treated with respect while asleep, feeding or playing is unlikely to deliver so much as a scratch.

Cats are pretty clever when it comes to looking after themselves; even when they look as though they are in trouble, they invariably aren't. Cats love to climb trees and can usually climb down just as easily; sometimes, however, the young or inexperienced cat may panic and get stuck, when it will need your help. Similarly, cats don't particularly like water and usually avoid it, but a curious cat may occasionally get itself into deep water.

CAT SAFETY

Keeping a cat safe from harm is the duty of every owner and, surrounded by so many dangers, we must do everything we can to minimize the risks to our pets.

In the case of a cat which is allowed outside, by far the greatest worry is that it may go missing and we all tend to think the worst when such a situation arises. However, should your cat disappear for a longer period than is normal, be sure you make a methodical search before becoming too alarmed. You may believe he is still outside; however, it could be that he has returned home without your knowledge and has slipped into the clothes-airing cupboard for a nap or is curled up under a duvet. Make sure you look in such likely places before commencing your search in earnest. When checking outside, it is worth looking in sheds and garages and other outhouses to see if someone has inadvertently shut the cat away. Also check with neighbours in case the cat has slipped unnoticed through an open doorway or window and into their house. Finally, search the whole neighbourhood, remembering to look up trees; cats love to explore high places and then become too afraid to jump down from them.

If, after a day, your cat has still not

RIGHT

RIGHT
*Young kittens may not be
as wise or careful as
older cats, so keep
upstairs windows shut
until he is older.*

OPPOSITE
*Once your kitten has had
his vaccinations, he can
begin to explore the
world outside. Keep a
close eye on him until
you are confident that he
is able to fend for
himself.*

arrived home, you may wish to contact
the police, animal rescue centres and
veterinary surgeries, who may have
picked him up because he has strayed or
has had an accident.

Tagging
Have your cat tagged in order to set your
mind at rest. Attach a metal tag which
carries your name and address to an
elasticated or quick-release collar, when
anyone finding him can contact you
immediately. Do not put your cat's name
on the tag, as a thief could well use it to
call him to entice him away. As a back-up
to the collar tag, you may wish to
consider an identity chip. A microchip is
inserted into the loose skin at the back of
the neck when it can be scanned and a
number exclusive to your pet can then be
read off on a display unit. All vets and
animal rescue centres have the equipment
to read these identichips and numbers are
listed on a national data base, which will
also hold the owners' details. It is also a
good idea to add a tag to the cat's collar
confirming that it is so equipped. The
process of inserting the identichip is
quick and painless and can be carried out
at your local veterinary surgery.

The Danger Outside
Most people feel at their happiest when
they can see their cat happily perched

Accidental injury is one of the hazards of an outside life, and broken glass, barbed wire and heavy traffic can all take their toll. It is a good idea to take out veterinary insurance to help pay for any costly emergencies.

on a fence or ledge in their own back garden. However, there are dangers lurking everywhere and responsible owners must be vigilant at all times. Cats are curious creatures and addicted to climbing, jumping onto window ledges, up trees and onto roofs and they will happily scale walls and fences. Inevitably, they may overstretch their limits when they will be too frightened to climb down. Be ready to rescue your pet in a situation such as this, and keep a step-ladder handy for the purpose.

It is commonly believed that cats do not like dogs and vice versa, and it is true that they sometimes prefer to steer clear of one another. However, there is always the time when an overconfident or unsuspecting cat will arrive face-to-face with a dog, perhaps in next door's garden. Nine times out of ten the confrontation will result in the cat escaping over a fence or wall, leaving the dog to his own devices. Occasionally, however, a skirmish may result in one or both animals being hurt. If you suspect your cat has been injured by a dog, seek veterinary attention immediately as a bite may have caused some internal damage which is not immediately apparent.

Cats also occasionally fight among themselves, and injuries are unfortunately quite common, particularly in neighbourhoods where there is a large cat population. Being territorial, cats like to regularly patrol their area to ward off other cats which are trying to encroach onto their patch. Neutered animals are less territorial and will be unlikely to get into a fight. It therefore best to have your animal neutered if he is allowed to wander, as bites can become easily infected. If it apparent that he has been fighting, check the coat carefully for deep bites which may need to be looked at by a vet.

When choosing plants for your garden it is just as well to concentrate ones which you know to be safe for animals. While it is rare for a cat to be poisoned by a plant, there are exceptions to every rule. Plants such as clematis, lupins, rhododendrons and lily-of-the-valley are just some examples that should be avoided. Poisoning can also occur due to a cat consuming garden chemicals. It is preferable to avoid the use of slug pellets which are harmful both pets and wild life, although there are special ones which reportedly do little harm. Other pesticides and herbicides can also be lethal to animals so use them sparingly if you have to, and keep them in a shed or cupboard which can be locked.

Ponds and swimming pools are an [ser]ious hazard, particularly to young or [ex]perienced cats. Should a cat fall into [wat]er, it is important that there is an [easy] exit as it is very easy for a cat to [dro]wn. Fortunately, they do not like [wat]er and tend to avoid it.

You may prefer your cat to remain [with]in the confines of your garden; this [is a] very tall order as cats are extremely [goo]d at climbing. It may be that you are [wor]ried about busy traffic in the vicinity, [or e]ven theft. A very high fence with the [top] sloping inward can be a deterrent, but it may be necessary to enclose the whole garden with a run constructed from wire netting.

Safety in the Home

Even though we tend to worry more when our cat is outside, there are precautions to be taken to ensure that the inside of the house is safe. We already know how agile cats are and are frequently surprised by their ability to climb and jump to any height they choose. For this reason you have to make your house cat-proof at all levels.

LEFT
Many prescription drugs have a sugary coating and may attract a cat. Keep all drugs, chemicals and poisons locked securely away.

Beware of open upstairs windows. Even though it is unlikely that a cat will try to jump out, it may inadvertently fall. Balconies are also lethal and if you live in a high-rise building you should forbid your cat the balcony unless it has been specially adapted to make it thoroughly safe.

The kitchen is particularly hazardous: do not allow your cat onto the worktops. This is not only dangerous, it is also unhygienic. Knives, boiling kettles, hotplates, hot irons and chemicals used in the kitchen are all potentially lethal. Beware of washing machines and tumble dryers. Check that they do not contain a sleeping or inquisitive cat before switching them on.

In the rest of the house, anything

FAR LEFT
The house can be a potentially dangerous place for a cat, particularly the kitchen. Don't leave boiling pans or kettles unattended – shut the cat out of harm's way. This cat is in no danger; the ornaments on the window sill are a different matter!

Some houseplants are poisonous, and as cats enjoy chewing them, it is advisable to remove them out of harm's way.

electrical is a potential danger and wires should be tidied away in order to prevent a playful cat from chewing through them. Any type of fire, whether open or otherwise, is a hazard. Remember that poisonous plants are not only encountered in the garden: many of our common houseplants, such as ivies, are poisonous and a bored cat may decide to attack a plant with unfortunate results. If in doubt, banish plants from your house altogether.

In the bathroom, make sure the lid of the lavatory bowl is always kept closed as cats are sometimes tempted to drink from them and could fall inside and drown or be poisoned by chemical cleaners. Never leave a bath filled with hot water unattended, not even for a minute.

OUTDOOR SAFETY CHECK LIST

Remove poisonous plants

•

Try to avoid living near busy traffic

•

Avoid ponds and cover swimming pools when not in use

•

Keep garden shed doors locked

•

Lock away garden fertilizers and weedkillers

SAFETY IN THE HOME CHECK LIST

Keep all poisonous plants out of reach

•

Keep dangerous household products locked away

•

Unplug appliances not in use and remove dangling cables

•

Protect open fires with a fireguard

•

Keep cats and kittens away from upstairs windows

•

Keep cats out of the kitchen when cooking

Be aware of the dangers that lurk outside and that a wandering cat may inadvertently become imprisoned in an outhouse or garden shed.

Cats and kittens require a well balanced diet in order to stay happy and healthy.

FEEDING YOUR CAT

Cats are essentially carnivores, but a good diet should be a balanced combination of proteins, fats, minerals, vitamins and water. It is essential that cats are fed meat, as they cannot survive on a vegetarian diet. In fact a cat's dietary requirements are quite complex and it is not necessarily a good idea to feed it entirely on fresh meat which may lead to a deficiency in certain proteins or trace elements. However, if this is your choice, you must feed an additional vitamin and mineral supplement. These supplements can be harmful if overfed, so check the instructions carefully. By far the best way of feeding your cat is to give it a combination of fresh and formulated foods. This will ensure a balanced diet and avoid boredom from having to eat the same food over and over again.

Pet food manufacturers make sure all the elements necessary for good health are contained within their products and instructions on the label will advise you on amounts to feed which are relevant to your animal's weight and age. There are many different formulated feeds available, ranging from those suitable for kittens and adolescents to special ones for older cats. Ultimately, careful feeding will be reflected in your cat's appearance. A well fed cat has a

Canned and specially formulated cat foods are ideal because they contain all the correct nutrients. When feeding fresh food, however, it is often easy for a cat to miss out on vital vitamins and minerals which it would naturally get from chewing up all parts of a natural prey.

The cat opposite is a picture of health and vitality.

gleaming coat, bright eyes and a lithe, well muscled body.

In their wild state, cats are hunters, catching and eating a variety of small animals. They usually consume the prey in its entirety, which includes muscles, bones, stomach contents and even the head. Provided that you feed your cat the correct balance of food in small regular meals, you will be duplicating his natural feeding habits.

Water

A vital component in sustaining all life, water is also necessary to ensure the correct functioning of the cat's digestive system, particularly when feeding it dried foods. Make sure clean, fresh water is available at all times.

Milk

Cow's milk can upset the digestion but if your cat loves milk, special lactose-reduced brands are available which will be easier for him to digest. Do not offer milk as a substitute to water.

Canned Foods

Most cats are fed canned foods and there are many different brands and flavours from which to choose. As a general rule, try to feed the better quality ones which, though more expensive, will be more nutritious and

BELOW

No one is quite sure why cats eat grass; it could be a way of obtaining vitamins and minerals, though it is usually vomited up afterwards. It could simply be a way of clearing out the system.

contain less cereal to bulk them out. Keep your cat interested by changing types regularly and follow the feeding instructions on the label.

Dried Foods

Nearly all cats love dried foods which are less messy alternatives to canned foods; there is also less wastage as the food can be left out all day without it spoiling. They are complete foods, which means that you do not have to worry about keeping the diet balanced. The crunchy texture may help keep teeth in good condition, but a large cooked bone is always better. It is essential that when feeding dried foods, a clean supply of water is made freely

GOLDEN RULES OF FEEDING

Feed little and often. At least 2–3 meals a day is best. Allow access to fresh water at all times.

•

Give food taken from the refrigerator time to warm up or, if freshly cooked, allow it to cool down to room temperature before feeding.

•

Watch your cat's weight. As a rule, cats do not suffer from obesity, but if you suspect he is putting on weight, ask your vet to provide a diet sheet.

•

Only give special lactose-reduced milk formulated for cats.

•

Kittens need special attention and must be fed more regularly than adults. Stick to specialist feeds and follow manufacturers' instructions carefully.

•

Elderly cats need food that is more easily digestible, e.g. fish, rabbit and chicken, and meals need to be smaller

and more frequent. If using a formulated food, follow the instructions carefully.

•

If your cat is a fussy eater, introduce more variety into the diet and try to discover his favourite foods.

•

If your cat is ill, ask your vet what you should be feeding him.

•

For reasons of hygiene, keep bowls and utensils used for animals separate from those for human beings.

•

All small bones must always be removed from food.

•

Do not feed foods which have been formulated for other animals, e.g. for dogs.

•

Use clean bowls for each meal.

•

Remove food which has been left uneaten and has become stale.

available as little or no moisture is present in these types of foods.

Fresh Food

Cats love to eat freshly cooked meat and

fish and you could offer fresh food a twice-weekly alternative to formulate foods, in which case you can be sure a healthy balance. Make sure all foo properly cooked to avoid stomach upsets and take care to remove all small bones. Large cooked bones are great for the teeth and will help prevent the build-up of tartar. The occasional can of tuna or sardines will also be a welcome treat.

Grass

Anyone who knows cats will have noticed that they occasionally eat grass. It is thought that they do this to obtain folic acid and certain minerals, but cats usually vomit afterwards so it may be nature's way of cleaning out the system or of getting rid of fur balls. Cats which are permanently indoors can be given a tray of grass grown especially for them in a seedbox.

It is most important that kittens are given a well balanced diet for healthy growth. Formulated foods specially produced for kittens are recommended.

Marking out its territory is an important part of a cat's life, when it releases a strong scent detectable only to other cats which either attracts or warns them away.

CAT BEHAVIOUR

Cats are fascinating creatures, and even though they have adapted easily to a domesticated life, they still retain many of the traits of their wild ancestors and will readily revert to a feral state should the situation arise. Most of our domestic cats are well fed and watered but, even so, they still retain an atavistic instinct to hunt and continue to seek out prey, though now more for fun than necessity. For this, they remain well equipped with pointed teeth and razor-sharp claws; their eyesight is second to none and allows them to see in almost total darkness.

Spraying

This is the way a cat marks out its territory using its own urine. When a cat is urinating normally, it adopts a squatting position. However, when spraying, the cat's hindquarters are held high, and a jet of urine is directed at an object, usually a fence or a tree. All cats spray: it doesn't matter if they are male or female, neutered or unneutered, though unneutered animals are likely to spray more. This type of behaviour enables cats to communicate with one another regarding territory, age and sex and the aim is to either attract or deter other cats to and from their territory. In general, spraying is only carried out

outside; however, in certain situations, usually when the cat is under stress, spraying can occur indoors; however, this is short-lived once the source of the stress has been removed. A new pet added to the family, or a move to another house, are typical situations which may well be stressful to a cat.

Rubbing Against Objects

Cats mark their territory in other ways and one of the most appealing is the way they rub themselves against us. Cats have glands in the head, body and tail that exude a strong odour which other cats can smell, but which is fortunately imperceptible to us. When cats mark their territory in this way, they are telling other cats that you are their property and are out of bounds. Cats do this everywhere, on you and your furniture, in the home and on fences, trees and plants outside.

Scratching

Cats love to sharpen and manicure their claws on trees and other objects that will allow them to get really stuck in. Some cats greatly prefer your furniture and carpets, which should be discouraged and a scratching post provided. Cats have scent glands on their paw pads so, as they scratch, they are also releasing an odour to mark their territory.

Cats have two reasons for scratching. One is to keep the claws sharp, and can be achieved by scratching your furniture and carpets, which should be discouraged. The other is another way of marking out territory, which the cat does by means of scent glands in its paw pads.

RIGHT

This cat is assuming an aggressive stance to warn another cat off his territory. All cats fight, but you can reduce this by having your own cat neutered. Cats also tend to fight at night, so keeping him in will also help.

FAR RIGHT

Cats which are well fed don't hunt because they are hungry but because they have an irresistible urge to stalk prey. This also explains why they cruelly play with their prey rather than going for a quick kill.

Fighting

Because they are territorial animals, cats will often come into conflict with others of their species. Most prefer to avoid confrontation and neutering reduces the will to fight. Cats adopt various postures, depending upon whether they are showing aggression or submission. A puffed-up coat and tail will hopefully make an aggressor retreat and a cat which rolls over onto its back is indicating that it does not wish to fight. Fights between cats mainly take place at night, so avoid them happening by keeping your cat locked in. If you think

he may have been involved in a fight, check him over carefully for injury.

Hunting

Domestic cats do not hunt because they are hungry but because they enjoy stalking prey and their method is very similar to the way in which big cats and wildcats hunt. Using all their senses to track down their prey, they stalk silently through undergrowth, along branches, or crouch close to the ground. Once in range, in a split second they pounce to trap their victim. It is well known that domestic cats play with their prey rather

than making a quick kill. This is possibly because they are driven to hu by instinct and not hunger, in which case the kill would be quicker and mo decisive.

Why Cats Purr

It is not fully understood why cats pu although it is generally thought to sho contentment, even though cats have b known to purr when in pain. Purring almost exclusive to felines, but hyena make a similar sound when suckling. When we stroke a cat, purring usuall begins straight away. There is no

Like their larger cousins in the wild, all cats like to hunt, and kittens play in order to sharpen their wits and prepare themselves for this eventuality.

scientific explanation, but one theory is that the noise comes from the larynx, produced by muscles which close the vocal cords, which open when a rush of air passes through, causing this peculiar resonance.

The Senses

The cat has enhanced senses of sight, hearing and smell which make it a successful hunter. Cats can just as easily thrive in the wild, surviving on the small animals and birds they catch with remarkable skill and dexterity. Moreover, the acuity of their senses are combined with an astounding athleticism. These abilities have been passed down from the domestic cat's wild ancestors, along with a compelling urge to hunt.

Sight A cat's eyes are not only beautiful and striking but are also highly adapted to its life as a hunter. They are particularly effective at night; the pupil has the ability to dilate more fully than ours, allowing more light to hit the sensitive retina at the back of the eye. This enables the cat to see well when engaged in its nocturnal prowlings.

Hearing Cats can not only hear much better than human beings, they also receive a wider range of sounds, including very high- and low-pitched

OPPOSITE
A cat's senses are extremely accute, particularly sight, hearing and smell, all contributing to make it an excellent hunter. I am sure that the mouse in the picture is a close friend!

TOP LEFT
With a larger olfactory organ than human beings, the cat has a powerful sense of smell, and can often be seen sniffing the air in the hope of detecting the presence of another cat or possible prey.

LEFT
A cat's eyesight is highly developed and perfectly adapted to its role as a predator, particularly when hunting at night, when it can focus on the smallest of objects and pounce on them with remarkable acuracy.

Cats are naturally clean animals and tend to cover their tracks after evacuating outside. Urinating indoors can be stress-related, maybe caused by the arrival of another pet or a new baby into the family. This should stop once everything has settled back to normal. However, make sure that your cat is not suffering from a bladder infection or kidney disease, as excessive urination may be a symptom of this.

noises imperceptible to us. Their ears can rotate though 180°, enabling them to locate the source of the tiniest movement in the undergrowth. Due to their excellent hearing, it is not surprising that cats flee when the vacuum cleaner is switched on or we drop a saucepan in the kitchen – the sound must be deafening to them. It is this acute hearing, coupled with excellent night vision, which makes the cat a masterful hunter, even of the smallest and fastest prey.

Smell A cat needs to sniff out its prey during hunting and its olfactory lobes are very well developed to perceive the faintest odour and also helps it to locate

other cats. Cats have an additional attribute which some other mammals have and occurs when the upper lip is curled up to allow more scent to reach Jacobson's organ in the mouth. This is known as 'flehming'. This particular organ is not vital to the domestic cat's survival, but to his wild cousins it can be the difference between life and death.

Behavioural Problems

Much of what we consider 'bad' behaviour may be normal in a cat, but has become exaggerated due to certain circumstances such as stress. Spraying in the house is a case in point when a cat is feeling insecure and it is possible that he needs to mark his domiciliary territory to re-establish his confidence. Cats cannot be taught how to behave and they are not affected by punishment. The only way we can influence their behaviour is through tact and immediate action. Try to look at the problem from your cat's point of view, which may make you more sympathetic to the situation. However, never rule out a medical disorder, which could he the root cause of the problem; veterinary advice should be sought in the first instance if you are at all worried. Confident, happy cats are less likely to become a problem, so it is important to socialize them from the time they are kittens when the incidence

of unacceptable behaviour will be kept to a minimum. Kittens should be allowed to interact with other animals, children and adults. In this way, you can rule out situations which could alarm a cat once it is older and more set in its ways.

Spraying and Urinating Indoors It is important to know the difference between spraying and urinating. Spraying is the way in which territory i marked and usually occurs out-of-doors However, once subjected to stress, it ma begin to feel threatened enough to caus it to mark its territory in the home. A new pet or baby in the house may well trigger this behaviour and a change of circumstance such as moving house or the arrival of new carpet or furniture may also have this effect. However, spraying usually ceases once the cat ha regained confidence. If he shows signs insecurity, try to avoid situations whic might upset him if at all possible. If he entire, consider having him neutered this will possibly solve the problem. Your vet can also prescribe either hormone treatment or anti-anxiety dr which are also known to be efficaciou

Urinating indoors can also be stre related. However, it is important that make sure that your cat is not sufferi from a bladder infection or certain ot

ases. Check him out with your vet
use cats are naturally clean animals
would not normally indulge in such
viour without cause. Make sure he
a fresh, clean, litter tray in a
ded part of the house as cats feel at
most vulnerable when evacuating.
check that he is happy with the
d of litter in his tray and try
ging it if not. Make sure you
oughly clean all areas which have
soiled, as the slightest trace of a
ering odour may encourage him to
fend. This applies to sprayers too.

ession Cats which have been
active as youngsters often continue
boisterous behaviour into
thood, which is alarming for their
ers who may suffer bites and
ches as a consequence. A pouncing
n is cute and harmless; however,
behaviour must not be allowed to
inue in adulthood. Cats which
ch and bite must be given plenty of
to play with and if they persist must
colded sharply whenever they re-
d.

ving Fabrics This is a strange habit,
common in the Oriental breeds
as Siamese and Burmese, which
lop the habit of chewing and
lowing woollen clothing due to

stress, leaving large holes in garments.
This is an undesirable as well as an
unhealthy habit, as wool can build up in
the cat's intestine and require surgery to
remove it. A solution to the problem is
to remove materials which the cat finds
attractive and to provide it with plenty
of toys to play with as a distraction.

Nervous Grooming This can occur in
any breed, but is most common in the
Siamese. The cat becomes an obsessional
groomer and doesn't seem to be able to
stop licking itself, which causes sore,
bleeding patches to develop. This is very
difficult to cure, although some owners
have managed to break the habit by
putting orange juice on the coat to
discourage the cat from licking it. In
severe cases, and as a last resort,
tranquillizers may be prescribed.

Eating Houseplants Cats like eating
grass in small amounts and in some
instances may attack your houseplants as
a grass substitute. This is usually a
problem confined to cats which are kept
indoors all the time, but all cats can
develop the habit. If this becomes a
problem, it should be discouraged, as
many of the plants we keep inside are
poisonous and dangerous if eaten. Even
if the plant is not poisonous, the foliage
can be almost completely destroyed by a

persistent animal; try to keep plants
confined to a room which is out of
bounds and do not ever leave your cat
alone in a room with them. Try growing
a tray of grass especially for your cat to
chew.

Refusing Food One of the most alarming
things an animal lover can imagine is the
prospect of their pet refusing food and
losing weight as a result. Cats are the
worst offenders and while many seem to
eat anything, others are so fussy that
their food must be exactly of the right
kind and at the correct temperature,
otherwise they will simply not eat it. If
this is the case, it is important that you
try to discover your cat's preferences in
order to keep it happy and healthy.

*While some cats will eat
anything, others are
naturally fussy, which
can be worrying and
frustrating. Offer your cat
a variety of foods until
you find something he
likes. You may have to
resort to feeding fresh
food such as chicken or
fish.*

Scratching at furniture and carpets is a big problem and you should discourage this type of behaviour from an early age. Admonishing your cat with a stern NO every time he offends may help, but the instinct remains very strong. A better solution is to exclude him from rooms which contain your most valuable furnishings.

Remember that cats like to eat little and often food that is fresh and at room temperature. The fussiest may refuse formulated foods and you may therefore have to feed freshly cooked food; there are very few cats which will refuse a piece of fresh fish or chicken. A diet consisting of fresh foods will require added supplements to make sure all the vital nutrients are present (see Feeding, pages 398–403).

Scratching Furniture The tendency to scratch has the dual purpose of marking territory and sharpening claws. Most cats which are allowed outside have a favourite tree or post which they use for the purpose, and cats that are never allowed out can be provided with a scratching post. However, this strong instinctual behaviour can sometimes be transferred to the furnishings in your home and can quickly get out of control when carpets, sofas and curtains are damaged beyond repair. If caught early enough, you may be able to deter your cat with a firm NO every time he offends, but it may persist when you are absent from the scene. A way of avoiding this happening is to exclude him from certain rooms when you are out of the house; another way is to choose soft furnishings which are unattractive to cats, e.g. leather or vinyl.

Stalking Birds Cats are partly responsible for the decreasing number of songbirds, and owners are driven to despair by what they see as a cruel trait in their pets. Cats love to stalk any kind of prey, but it seems that birds attract them most, possibly because of the way they dart and flutter. Some cats actually eat their prey, while others bring them home as gifts to their horrified owners. If you consider that your cat's hunting habits have gone too far, you can frustrate him by attaching a bell to an elasticated collar to warn potential victims of his approach. This

Cats have an overwhelming urge to stalk prey and birds seem to attract them most. Cats are contributing to the dwindling numbers of songbirds, much to the horror of their owners. Try to deter them as much as possible; fit your cat's collar with a bell which will warn birds of his approach and don't have a bird table or feed the birds in you garden as you will be putting them in further danger.

is really only a half measure as the problem seems impossible to cure completely, though it may diminish as the cat approaches old age.

The Timid or Nervous Cat It is difficult to restore confidence to nervous cats. Some cats which have been timid as kittens grow into timid adults, some do not, and it is not necessarily the case that cats that have been cruelly treated when young grow up to be insecure. Whatever the case, you need patience, tact and understanding if you wish to improve matters. In extreme cases, symptoms of anxiety are panting, shedding fur and crouching low to the ground, and many cats simply bolt for a hiding place once they find themselves in a stressful situation. Provide your cat with a quiet place where he can get himself out of the way and sleep. When he ventures out, make sure you remain quiet and calm. Do not try to grab or pick him up, but allow him to come to you. Extend your hand and allow him to sniff it before giving him a gentle stroke and reassuring him calmly in a gentle tone of voice. Offer a few titbits which will encourage him to come to you. In time, you may be able to instil more confidence into him and thereby increase his overall quality of life.

The Straying Cat A cat which has become accustomed to straying from home for long periods is a constant source of anguish to its owner, who seems to spend most of his time calling and scouring the neighbourhood for his pet. Unneutered cats need a larger territory in which to roam and neuterin may be a solution to the problem. Try feeding your cat at the same time each day. This way, you establish a routine and he will know to come home at mealtimes. Keeping him in at night wil also help the situation and will save yo from having a sleepless night worrying about him. In severe cases, also shut him in for periods during the day, whi may establish a more home-based lifestyle.

The ultimate way of controlling yo cat's tendencies to roam is to fence yo garden in such a way that he cannot escape. This can be done inexpensivel with chicken wire or plastic-coated w mesh. If you already have a high fenc extending its height is an easy matter, using wooden batons screwed togethe make a frame construction before fixi it to the fence. Tack the wire loosely position to cover the frame, using sm fencing staples and allowing about a to overhang along the top; this will d most cats from jumping over. Check ground level along the boundary, locking up any gaps as you go.

The alternative to this is to construct a cat run using similar materials. Ideally, the run should be connected to the house, enabling the cat to come and go as he pleases through a cat flap. The advantage of this arrangement is that you can also keep his litter tray, feeding bowls and other equipment outside, which will keep your house cleaner and odour-free. If the cat run is positioned a distance away from the house, be careful when transporting him to it in case he escapes. If you think this possible, always use a cat carrier.

Cats are timid or nervous for various reasons. They may have had an accident which has destroyed their confidence, or have been previously ill-treated, or they may simply have been born that way. You can improve matters by being patient and understanding and by providing your cat with a quiet, calm environment to which to live.

LEFT
Most cats, like this inquisitive little kitten, will wander off from time to time, but they are usually not too far away and will come to your call. Some, however, make a regular habit of disappearing for long periods of time. You may be able to curb this by establishing a routine, i.e. keeping him indoors at night and at certain times during the day. Alternatively, you may have to fence him in.

ON THE MOVE

At some time or other in your cat's life he will have to travel, at least once a year to the vet for his annual booster and, if you like to take a holiday, to a boarding cattery.

Travelling

Generally speaking, cats are not good travellers, though you will find that those which have travelled regularly from an early age adapt better to the natural movements of vehicles and aircraft. For most journeys you will need a well constructed cat carrier containing plenty of comfortable bedding. If the journey is likely to be a long one, you will also need to line it with newspaper in case the cat vomits or has diarrhoea. Make sure you take plenty of cleaning materials in case they are needed to clear up after an accident and provide plenty of clean, fresh water. If your cat is prone to vomiting, do not feed him immediately prior to a journey, but make sure you give him a small meal earlier in the day. In the case of a very nervous traveller, it may be necessary to consult your vet who may prescribe sedatives. However, do not administer any drug without veterinary advice.

Do not be tempted to allow your cat out of his carrier in the course of a

journey, as once out he may panic, causing possible distraction to the driver of the vehicle. In hot weather, take extra precautions that the animal does not become overheated. Make sure there is adequate ventilation and under no circumstances leave your cat unattended in a car.

Some cats begin to associate being put in a carrier with unpleasant experiences, such as visiting the vet or travelling in the car, so that whenever the carrier is produced he may try to flee. In such a case, it is a wise precaution to close cat flaps, doors and windows first and restrict the cat to one room in the house before placing him in

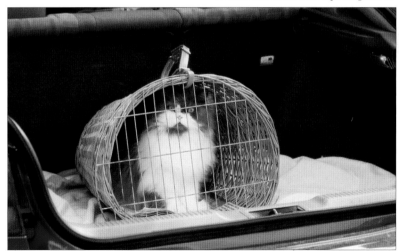

LEFT

As as rule, cats don't like travelling at all. However, providing them with a sturdy carrier filled with comfortable bedding will go a long way to ease the situation and prevent them from becoming too alarmed.

BELOW LEFT

Always secure you cat in a sturdy carrier placed on a flat surface and tied firmly down in case of accident. Never let a cat run loose inside a car; even if a person is holding him, he could still break free and cause considerable havoc.

When moving house it is advisable to keep your cat indoors for at least two weeks so that he can become used to his new surroundings and less likely to run off in panic.

Moving House

Moving to a new house is a traumatic experience and it is easy to forget your cat's special needs at this difficult time. Cats do not relish changes of environment or their routine disturbed, so it is up to you to make the process go as smoothly as possible.

For a few days leading up to the event, allow your cat to become accustomed to one particular, quiet room in your house. Lock him in that room for a few hours each day when he will become accustomed to the routine. On the day of the move, lock him away in his room before the chaos commences and ensure that all family members and the removal team know that they must not enter until last thing – put a notice on the door to discourage entry. Once the whole house has been cleared, carefully transfer your cat to his carrier taking his bed, water and feed bowls and any other paraphernalia, and transport him to the new house in a manner like to create the least disturbance. Once there, set him up in a similar quiet room accompanied by his toys, bed and familiar objects from the former house. Make sure all windows are closed to avoid him bolting and ensure that no one is likely to open the door.

Once the process of removal is complete and all the furniture is in

the carrier. When doing this, make sure you hold him gently but firmly, as he may attempt to wriggle out of your grasp. Make sure you close the carrier door as quickly as possible without causing alarm and double check that the catch is fastened to prevent the cat from escaping in a strange place, resulting in a lost and very frightened animal.

When taking your cat abroad, not only should you ensure that he will be comfortable on the journey, but you should also check out border restrictions and any other problems which may occur. Many countries and states restrict entry to avoid the spread of disease. If entry is permitted, it is likely that proof of vaccination as well as identity will be needed. In all cases, make sure you familiarize yourself with all requirements some months prior to departure. If you are travelling by air, contact the airline beforehand, which will advise you on equipment and other documentation you may require. In Britain, for example, inoculation against rabies was once only used on animals intended for export but now that quarantine regulations have been changed it is mandatory.

and the removal team have departed, you can begin to allow your cat restricted access to other rooms in the house. If you permit him to explore just a few rooms at a time, you will avoid confusing and alarming him. Most cats will have calmed down within a few days and will soon assume the run of the entire house. However, at this early stage, it is vital that you do not allow him outside, as being unfamiliar with his new surroundings he may run away and not know how to return. Confine him to the house for at least two weeks before letting him outside, by which time you can be sure that the cat now knows where he lives.

When you first let him outside, make sure you keep an eye on him or even accompany him into the garden, as this will reassure him. At first, let him outside before he has been fed, which will get him into the habit of returning home for meals. Eventually, he will move out his new territory and make new acquaintances; fortunately, cats adapt relatively quickly to new surroundings.

There are some who may wish to avoid putting their cat through the whole trauma of moving by boarding it in a cattery before packing up, and reintroducing it to the new house once the process has been completed.

After two weeks, allow your cat to explore a little further under your supervision. This cat is sitting by an open window taking in the air and surveying his new territory.

Soon your cat will have completely forgotten his old home and will have settled down happily in his new one.

Catteries

Most cats, at some stage or another during their lives, need to be boarded in a cattery, and vets or friends will often be able to make recommendations. However, it is still wise to visit the cattery personally prior to making a booking to check out its suitability. Reputable catteries are likely to welcome an inspection and will provide a guided tour. During inspection, make sure you ask to see the price list, ascertaining any hidden extras or insurances which may be necessary. If you intend to travel during the peak holiday period, book your cat in well in advance, or as soon as your trip is confirmed. Catteries can quickly fill up in the summer months and it can be very worrying and disappointing when you discover that the better ones are already fully booked.

The cattery should be immaculately clean, well maintained, and of sturdy construction. All the runs, beds and equipment should have been disinfected between use to avoid the spread of infection, and for the same reason cats should be kept apart. Bedding material should be disposable. The cattery must be secure enough to ensure no cat can escape and the enclosed area should have at least two sets of doors to be doubly sure. In winter, heating should be provided in the sleeping areas.

Proprietors of reputable establishments will always check that a cat's vaccination record is up to date before accepting it; so never allow vaccinations to lapse. On arrival, you will be asked to fill out a registration form and also a list of your pet's likes and dislikes as well as any food preferences he may have. You will be asked to provide an emergency contact number for the period that you are away. You may also be asked to provide your own vet's name and address.

It may be permissible to leave your cat some of his favourite toys to reassure him while you are away. The first time you leave him at a cattery, he may initially appear distressed as you walk away. However, he will soon acclimatize to his new surroundings and in a short time will settle down. If you have two cats, they can be housed together in a shared pen which will ensure that both cats settle down very quickly.

When collecting your cat after a trip away, check him over for general health and examine him for parasites in particular, such as fleas. Even vaccinated cats can pick up minor colds and infections and if you think this may be the case, consult your vet immediately. Remember to ask the cattery proprietor how your cat has fared as you may wish to use the establishment again.

In rare cases, cats may fret to an unacceptable extent when you may have to obtain the services of a house-sitter while you are absent from home.

Grooming

Cats are fastidious creatures and naturally spend a good deal of their time grooming themselves. Because of this, there is a misconception that this is all they require. However, all cats benefit from a daily grooming session and provided that this has been done from an early age, will actually grow to enjoy the process. Grooming helps clean the coat and reveals evidence of parasites. It is also a good opportunity to check a cat's general state of health; anything you notice which worries you should be reported immediately to your vet.

Claws

As well as giving the body a thorough grooming, there are also other areas which require special attention. Cats which venture outside do not usually need their claws clipped, but some cats, particularly those confined to the house or elderly ones, may require regular attention. Also check cats which go outside for injuries. Make sure you use clippers which have been specially designed for the purpose. Only a small area of the claw should be removed, taking care not to cut into any sensitive parts. Ask your vet to guide you through the process before trying it yourself.

Eyes

Cats' eyes are invariably clear and bright,

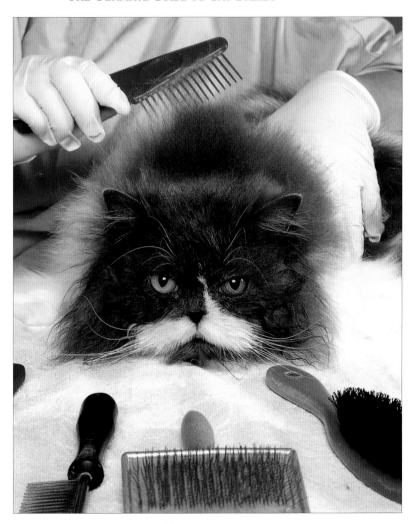

Grooming, particularly for longhaired cats, should be a daily routine. Not only will it prevent painful knots from forming, it also presents an opportunity to check your cat over for uninvited visitors such as fleas and ticks.

but sometimes they do require attention. Always take the greatest of care when cleaning around the eyes and use a piece of cotton wool dampened with a preparation designed for the purpose or water. Do not touch the eyeball directly and make sure no fibres enter the eyes.

Ears

Before cleaning, inspect the ears for disease. If there is a dark discharge, consult your vet. Clean the ears in the same way as the eyes and never use cotton buds or other implements.

Teeth

Older cats tend to suffer from gum problems which can be caused by a build-up of tartar on the teeth. It is therefore a good idea to accustom your cat to having his teeth cleaned from an early age. It is not necessary to do this every day, weekly will suffice. Use a small soft toothbrush and a specially formulated toothpaste for cats to gently clean the teeth. If this causes distress, try a cotton bud and toothpaste which is less disturbing.

Grooming the Coat

Whatever coat type your cat has, whether short, long, fluffy or double-layered, there is a comb for the purpose. Longhaired cats require rather more

attention and will need a daily grooming session. For shorthaired varieties, grooming is not so vital, although many owners groom daily because their cats enjoy it so much.

First use a soft brush and once the knots are removed the coat can be combed through. Discourage the cat from turning the process into a game. If the coat has become matted and you feel you cannot remove the mats through ordinary grooming, you may need to have them removed by your veterinary surgeon. Don't allow the coat to get into this state in the first place.

OPPOSITE
Shorthaired cats only require a quick brush over a few times a week, as the coat is not prone to matting. However, this regular grooming helps keep the skin and coat healthy and gleaming.

LEFT
Start cleaning your cat's teeth from an early age – weekly is sufficient. If your cat protests, and makes the task impossible, letting him gnaw on a lightly cooked chop bone will help to keep them clean.

RIGHT

*Most or all of the tools
on this page are required
to keep the longhaired
cat's coat in good
condition. For a
shorthaired cat,
a bristle brush is all that
is required.*

OPPOSITE

*The longhaired coat of
this Siberian Forest Cat
is shiny, tangle-free and
a joy to behold.*

GROOMING TOOLS

Fine-Toothed Comb Use this on shorthaired cats to remove dirt and stray fleas from the coat.

Wide-Toothed Comb Used on longhaired cats to remove tangles by combing the coat the wrong way and working on a small area at a time.

Dual Bristle and Pin Brush (bottom left) Use the bristle side on shorthaired cats

to lay the coat flat and add a final shine. Use the pin side to remove any residual tangles after combing through longhaired cats before finishing off with the bristle side.

Moulting Comb (above) Used to remove loose hair during moulting, it is used mainly on shorthaired cats, and very gently on thoroughly groomed longhaired cats.

Slicker Brush (above) A gentle way of removing tangles and mats from longhaired cats.

HEALTH MATTERS

Keeping your cat in peak condition should be your primary concern, as an unfit cat is an unhappy cat. Moreover, some disorders which affect cats can threaten other animals as well as people in the household. Provided your cat appears to be in good health, he will need a yearly check-up by a vet, which is a convenient time for his vaccination boosters to be given; following this, it is up to you to monitor his health. A healthy cat has an alert expression, bright eyes, a clean nose, ears and rear, a shiny coat and a lithe body. His disposition will be happy and playful and he will find it easy to relax and

sleep comfortably. A good appetite is also a sign of good health. If you think there may be something wrong, look at the skin and coat. Check the ears, eyes, nose and mouth. A runny nose may be a symptom of a cold or a weepy eye could indicate an infection. If you are in any doubt, seek veterinary assistance.

Common Problems

Fleas The flea is a common parasite, causing skin problems which result in constant scratching and washing which is distressful and which will impair the cat's overall condition. Usually fleas do not cause serious health problems; however, a severe allergic reaction can sometimes be triggered by their presence. Whatever the case, fleas do need controlling and must not be ignored; remember that warm weather increases flea numbers. If you suspect that your cat has fleas, pass a fine-toothed comb through his coat, particularly around the neck area, tipping it onto a piece of white paper. You will know you have a problem when tiny blackish flecks appear on the paper. These are flea droppings.

These days there are many different ways of controlling these pests which include injections and drugs. However, the most usual method is still an insecticide spray which should be recommended by your vet and obtained from his surgery. Always follow the directions carefully, as some sprays are harmful if breathed in or allowed to come into contact with human skin. Flea collars are a useful control method and provide a continuous flow of insecticide. Make sure the collar is elasticated and watch out for irritation as an allergic reaction can sometimes occur.

If fleas are present on your cat, they will also be in your house. Your vet will advise you on the types of sprays suitable for household use. Do not use these on your animals. Vacuuming carpets and soft furnishings regularly, while paying particular attention to all the nooks and crannies, and especially carpet edges, will help reduce the number of flea eggs in the home, serving to break the cycle of infestation. Controlling the incidence of tapeworms will also greatly help the situation (see page 429).

The presence of animals in the household calls for even greater hygiene. Get into the habit of keeping your house and your pets' sleeping areas spotlessly clean. This will reduce the likelihood of parasites such as fleas becoming a problem in the first place.

Kittens infested with fleas are a special case, so consult your vet who will prescribe the correct form of

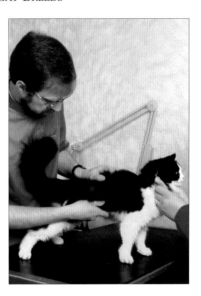

treatment. On no account apply a flea spray to a kitten under 7 weeks old. Instead, use a fine-toothed comb to remove the fleas and keep the bedding area scrupulously clean.

Ticks These are mainly a problem in rural areas where there is long grass, although they can be picked up anywhere. Ticks attach themselves by their mouth parts to the cat's head and neck area, feeding on the animal's blood for 4–5 days before dropping off. In some cases, a heavy infestation can cause anaemia. A bloated tick is grey-blue in

OPPOSITE LEFT
Being vigilant and noticing when things are not quite right will go a long way to keep your cat healthy and happy. Make sure that the eyes are bright, the nose and ears are clean and that the coat has a healthy sheen. Worm regularly and make sure that he is fully vaccinated and has his yearly booster.

OPPOSITE RIGHT
Excessive scratching can be a sign that your cat is suffering from a skin disorder or a flea infestation – not a serious problem if treated promptly.

ABOVE
Yearly booster vaccinations are vital, when your vet will also give your cat a general health check.

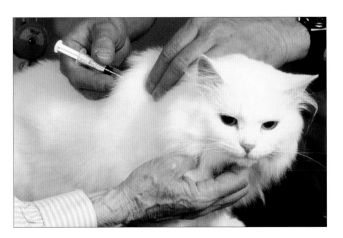

Vaccination is vital to guard against killer diseases such as feline infectious enteritis, feline leukaemia and cat flu.

colour and is the size of an apple pip. As spreaders of disease, it is important to rid the cat of ticks as soon as they are noticed. Do not attempt to pull them off – the mouth parts may remain in the cat causing infection. Instead, use a flea spray and after about 24 hours the dead tick can be removed using tweezers. Make sure the tick comes away from the skin intact and destroy it by burning.

Mange Fortunately, mange is a rare complaint in most countries. It is caused by a microscopic parasite called *notoedres cati*, which burrows under the cat's skin causing intense irritation. If you suspect your cat to be so afflicted, isolate him immediately and contact your vet.

Ear Mites These spread easily and are common in cats and kittens; your vet can prescribe ear drops to cure the complaint. The tiny mites cause irritation of the skin, resulting in head-shaking and the secretion of a dark-brown ear wax which is clearly visible inside the ear.

Fur Mites At first glance this appears to be dandruff spreading along the animal's back, but is in fact an infestation. Fortunately, it is a rare condition. Treat with a flea spray.

Harvest Mites These appear as tiny red dots and are usually found around the ears and between the toes. Treat with flea spray.

Ringworm This is a highly contagious fungal condition which can spread throughout many species of animals as well as human beings. The disease is characterized by scaly patches on the animal's skin. In humans, the condition is more easily recognized and takes the form of red circular patches. If you suspect ringworm, consult your vet immediately who will advise and prescribe treatment. The disease can also be spread through bedding, feeding bowls or almost anything with which the animal comes into contact; everything

must be burned once the infection has passed. When treating, wear gloves and thoroughly wash your hands afterwards. Treatment can take many weeks, which means that the animal must remain in isolation until completely cured.

Internal Parasites

Worms For cats which venture outside, and in particular those which hunt and eat their prey, worm infestations are not uncommon and most cats will be afflicted from time to time. Worms live inside the animal, feeding on digested food. Your vet can prescribe a regular worming programme to ensure that you cat is protected. Different species of worm are affected by different drugs making it essential that you seek veterinary advice.

Roundworms Kittens are most likely pick up roundworms, which are contracted through their mother's milk Diarrhoea or constipation, weight-loss and general deterioration in condition are all symptoms and the kitten may have a pot-bellied appearance. If they passed in the animal's stool the worm resemble lengths of white thread. As a riskier situation for a tiny kitten to ill, your vet should be consulted as as symptoms are recognized. In fact, kittens should be wormed regularly f

the age of 6 weeks and pregnant cats should also receive treatment. Your vet will prescribe a suitable worming programme.

Tapeworms These attach themselves to the wall of the host's gut and can grow very long. They are made up of egg-filled segments that separate off and are passed with the cat's motions. The first sign of infestation is when you discover a small, white, moving oblect attached to the cat's rear end. This is a segment which has broken away from the rest of the worm in the cat's gut. All cats should be wormed every 6 months and you will need special advice from your vet when worming kittens. It is important that your cat is regularly treated for fleas as they can cause re-infection. The tapeworm larvae develop within the flea which, if ingested by the cat when licking its fur, will cause a further infestation.

Toxoplasmosis *Toxoplasmas gondii* are microscopic intestinal parasites which use the cat as its primary host. They usually live in the bowel and shed their eggs which are passed in the cat's motions. An infected cat rarely shows symptoms but the disease is transmissible to humans and is very dangerous as it can cause damage to

Cats and kittens should be wormed regularly from 6 months onwards. Ask you vet to prescribe an effective product and make sure you follow the regime.

Fur balls are particularly common in longhaired cats, but the problem can be considerably alleviated by daily grooming, which will remove most of the loose hairs.

unborn children. It is most important that pregnant women do not touch cats' litter trays and the job of changing the litter is best left to others. However, whatever the circumstances, hygiene is of prime importance when cleaning up after any animal. Litter trays should be regularly disinfected and hands thoroughly washed. To keep matters in proportion, though, infection is rarely passed to human beings by pets, being more likely to occur through handling uncooked meats or dirty vegetables.

Other Conditions

Fur Balls When cats lick their fur to clean it, there is always a certain amount that is ingested. Some cats, particularly those with long fur, can swallow quite a lot and the loose hairs cause a matted ball within the stomach. Once the ball grows to a certain size, the cat will vomit it up. If your cat is prone to this condition, make sure he is groomed regularly, removing most of the loose hair before he has time to swallow it. If you are worried about the condition, consult your vet who will advise special treatment. A simple remedy you can use at home is to dose your cat with a fish oil or a small amount of olive oil to lubricate and soften the fur ball, which will more easily pass through the system.

Eye Conditions

Conjunctivitis Fortunately, this is a rare disease in cats and is usually caused by a scratch or a foreign body entering the eye. The infection causes the eye to become inflamed and if left untreated can become ulcerated. Consult your vet immediately.

Eye Injuries Most injuries to the eye area occur when cats fight. Provided that the wound is small and not actually in the eye, it will usually heal without problem. However, if the wound is deep close to or in the eye itself, it could be more serious and your vet should be consulted without delay.

Watery Eyes Some cats, particularly pedigree types, are susceptible to this condition which is usually caused by an overactive tear duct. However, if you suspect the watering is being caused by an irritation, a blocked tear duct, or other disease, or if the discharge is extensive, consult your vet immediately.

Conditions

Eyes (See page 428)

Infections The ear canal can become inflamed due to a fungus or bacteria or in some cases the introduction of a foreign body. If your cat continually scratches his ears or there is a discharge coming from them, consult your vet who will usually prescribe ear drops.

Haematoma A haematoma, or blood-filled blister, can develop on the cat's ear and is usually the result of having being scratched while fighting. As the ears are very sensitive, haematomas can be painful and will need draining as they will not disappear of their own accord. This should be carried out by your veterinary surgeon as soon as you notice the condition.

Mouth Conditions

Wildcats have a varied diet and much of the food they eat involves a good deal of chewing and gnawing, which cleans the teeth, strengthening them in the process. Many of the processed foods we feed today do not act as positively on the teeth and therefore it is not surprising that many of our domestic cats have gum and tooth problems.

All cats can suffer from dental problems. However, it is the older ones which are most susceptible and a build-up of plaque or tartar on the surface of the teeth can lead to infection and inflammation of the gums (gingivitis). Bad breath or problems with eating are signs that all is not well. Check your cat's teeth and gums regularly and accustom him to having his teeth cleaned weekly. Consult your vet if you are at all concerned.

Gingivitis This is an infection of the gums, the first sign of which is a red line of inflammation between tooth and gum. The condition is extremely painful and will require veterinary attention. Clean your cat's teeth and gums regularly. A lightly cooked chop bone is ideal for him to gnaw on and will help remove debris from the teeth and strengthen the gums.

Respiratory Problems At some point in their lives, nearly all cats present cold-like symptoms. Sneezing, coughing and laboured breathing are common signs,

Deposits of a light brown substance called tartar can build up on the teeth, leading to gum irritation and gingivitis.

but also watch for runny eyes and noses. Usually the condition is mild and disappears after a day or so. Should the symptoms persist or worsen drastically, however, veterinary attention should be sought immediately.

Feline Respiratory Disease (Cat Flu)
There are two respiratory diseases commonly known as cat flu, one being Feline Calici Virus (FCV) and the other Feline Viral Rhinotracheitis (FVR). The symptoms are fever, coughing and sneezing, runny eyes and nose. The condition may cause the cat to temporarily lose his appetite due to a reduction in his sense of smell. FCV can cause painful mouth ulcers, but it is FVR which is the most dangerous of the two types. The disease affects the nose, trachea and lungs and breathing can become very difficult. Kittens and older cats are particularly at risk as they may not have the stamina to recover. In any case of flu, attention should be sought as your vet may wish to prescribe antibiotics to limit the spread of a secondary bacterial infection. Flu patients require careful nursing and feeding as well as plenty of rest, and gentle bathing of the eyes and nose will make the cat feel more comfortable. Unfortunately, the virus can persist in the cat's system after recovery and should it

later fall ill or be under stress, the virus can be shed, infecting other cats.

As always, prevention is better than cure, so make sure your cat is vaccinated; all cats should be vaccinated as kittens at 9 to 12 weeks with a second vaccination one month later, and given regular boosters annually.

Chlamydial Disease This is a disease of the respiratory system and produces flu-like symptoms. The condition is quite rare, but more common where large numbers of cats are congregated together, as in breeding establishments. Even though the the risk is small, the disease is transmissible to human beings, so hygiene must be strictly observed when symptoms are present. Always wash your hands after handling an infected or suspected case. It is possible to vaccinate against the disease, so if you think your cat or cats are at risk, consult your vet.

Digestive Disorders
Feline Infectious Enteritis (FIE) This is a serious viral disease which is highly contagious and an infected cat is unlikely to recover. The virus affects the digestive tract and persistent vomiting, fever, bloody diarrhoea, depression and severe dehydration are the symptoms. Infected cats must be isolated at once and will require immediate veterinary

care when intravenous fluids will possibly be introduced. Treatment is rarely successful and in order to prevent further infection, your whole house will need to be decontaminated. Your vet will be able to advise you on this. If you intend to introduce a new cat into the environment, make sure it has been vaccinated for FIE at least two weeks previously. Vaccinations, with yearly boosters, are essential to prevent cats from contracting this terrible disease.

Feline Infectious Peritonitis (FIP) This can strike cats of any age, although younger ones are more susceptible and have less resistance. The virus which causes the disease is called Coronavirus (CoV). Many cats throw off the infection with few signs of the disease, but sadly some cats go on to develop the full-blown version which is fatal. The virus affects the abdominal cavity, liver, kidneys, brain and nervous system. There is no cure and no vaccine for this disease and therefore patients must be isolated before death to prevent infection from spreading. Fortunately, the virus is not very resilient and is easily destroyed through disinfection; it can only survive at room temperature for a couple of days.

Diarrhoea This has many causes, including a change in diet and a stressful situation. Mild diarrhoea will pass very quickly, however; if it persists longer than 24 hours, or is accompanied by vomiting or blood is present in the

stools, it could be a sign of a more serious disorder, so consult your vet immediately. During any case of diarrhoea, the most common complication is dehydration, so it is important to make sure fresh water is freely available at all times.

Constipation This is a common condition, but is more likely to afflict elderly cats. If you notice your cat straining to produce a motion, try to establish that it is a stool that he is trying to pass and not urine. A cat unable to pass urine should be treated as an emergency and immediate veterinary attention is essential. In mild cases you can treat constipation by feeding your cat oily fish or a little butter to help lubricate the digestive system. If, after 24 hours, the cat's bowels have still not moved, take it to the vet who may administer an enema.

FACTS ABOUT NEUTERING

Neutering is permanent sterilization; it involves the removal of the testicles in males and of the uterus and ovaries in females. It is now a very safe operation and causes little discomfort.

Benefits Neutering will benefit males and females far more that leaving them entire. It virtually eradicates the chances

of prostate and testicular cancers and modifies behavioural problems such as spraying, roaming and fighting. Females are unlikely to develop breast or uterine cancer, and unwanted gentlemen callers or the risk of pregnancy will no longer be a problem. Both males and females are less likely to stray, thereby reducing the risk of road and other accidents.

Veterinarians try to keep the cost of neutering down to a minimum to encourage people to have their pets neutered; if you still cannot afford this, there are organizations which offer very low-cost neutering.

Many thousands of unwanted cats are destroyed every year due to unplanned pregnancies. Reduce these numbers by having your cat neutered!

Your cat will, in fact, benefit from neutering, when behavioural problems such as spraying and aggression towards other cats will be considerably reduced.

FIRST AID

Cats are naturally inquisitive animals and often wander into danger, both inside the home and out of it. All owners of cats should be well prepared for potential emergencies and be ready to administer first aid which may be life-saving. When you first discover an injured animal, before touching it, make sure that you handle it in such a way as to avoid being bitten or scratched, as a frightened, injured cat is liable to behave out of character. Try to keep him as calm and as quiet as possible, when your first priorities will be to stop any bleeding and keep the animal breathing. Once stabilized, telephone the vet for advice, who will usually arrange for an immediate consultation. Wrap the injured animal in a blanket, keeping him secure, warm and quiet and get him to the vet as quickly but as safely as possible.

Bites During fights, cats often scratch and bite one another. If your cat returns home and is showing signs of severe injury, you will need to take him to the vet. However, in most cases the injuries will not be too severe but merely minor wounds. Unfortunately, when a cat is bitten by another, harmful bacteria in the saliva gets into the wound. As soon as you become aware of a bite, bathe it regularly with salt water to keep the injury clean while it heals. This will minimize the likelihood of infection. However, it is more likely that you will not be aware of the injury. It is only after a few days, after the surface of the wound has healed up, that an abscess may develop underneath. This causes swelling and severe pain at the site of the wound. Usually the abscess will burst open, leaving a gaping hole which will need to be bathed regularly with salt water; you will need to consult your vet who will usually prescribe antibiotics and may even stitch the wound. On discovering an abscess which has not burst, take the animal to the vet who will drain it and prescribe drugs.

Burns Cats usually steer clear of intense heat, but occasionally accidents do happen due to a spitting fire, or boiling water or hot fat spilling over. Apply cold, running water to the affected parts for several minutes before seeking immediate veterinary attention. Do no

Cats are by nature inquisitive creatures and despite their agility can occasionally get themselves into trouble. Accidents in the kitchen are usually burns-related, caused by hotplates and water boiling over. If your cat is accidentally burned, allow cold water to run over the affected parts and seek veterinary attention immediately.

pply anything else to the wound.

Chemical burns should be treated in he same way. Remember to protect your wn hands with rubber gloves when andling the patient. If the chemical is nown, it is important to report this formation to your vet as this will have bearing on his treatment of the injury.

Burns can also be caused by an ectric shock, usually caused when a cat ews through an electric cable, when it likely to suffer burns to the mouth. If u discover that your cat has been ectrocuted, switch of the current before ing anything else. This will make the a safe for both you and your patient. he cat is not breathing, he may require rdio-Pulmonary Resuscitation (page), followed by veterinary attention.

Sunburn is a common hazard in ny climes and prevalent everywhere ats with white or light-coloured ears. ke sure you use a sunblock especially nulated for cats with a very high sun ection factor. If you find that the ears being repeatedly burned, you may to keep him in when it is cularly sunny outside. If the dition seems severe, consult your vet ediately.

ing There are any number of ts around the house and garden a an choke on, but chicken and fish

Drowning is fortunately rare in cats, as they have a natural antipathy towards water. However, they have been known to fall into ponds and rivers, so make yourself familiar with the resuscitation techniques on page 438.

RIGHT

This cat is not very well at all, and appears listless and thoroughly subdued. He has been placed in intensive care and has been put on a drip to help his recovery.

OPPOSITE

Cats usually know what they can and cannot eat. However, the most common form of poisoning is when a cat eats a rodent which has itself been poisoned.

bones are perhaps the most common. If he appears distressed, is pawing at his mouth, or even attempting to vomit, this should lead you to suspect that something is lodged in his throat. Before attempting to remove the object, you should first restrain him by wrapping him firmly in a towel. Using a pair of tweezers, try to remove the object, but if you cannot, seek veterinary attention immediately.

Drowning It is rare for a cat to drown as they do not like water and will tend to avoid it. However, there is always an exception to every rule and cats occasionally fall into ponds and rivers. Once this happens, the lungs will quickly fill with water and the cat will stop breathing. After retrieval, and if the cat remains motionless, hold it upside-down by its back legs and swing it gently in front of you and back between your legs. Take care not to let the head touch the ground which could cause further injury. If the cat is still not breathing, use cardio-pulmonary resuscitation (page 438).

Road Traffic Accidents Every day, busy streets claim the lives of a large number of cats and injure even more, so if you live in a built-up area you should be mindful of all the dangers. If, in the harrowing situation that your cat is

discovered at the roadside showing signs of injury, you should treat this as an emergency; it is important that you get the patient directly to a veterinary hospital without delay. External injuries are often immediately obvious and first aid to arrest bleeding is essential. Internal injuries may not be visible at all, but your vet will thoroughly check the cat over once he arrives in the hospital. Construct a makeshift stretcher from a coat and very carefully transfer the cat onto it, avoiding sudden movements. Keep him warm and quiet

and the head slightly lower than the rest of the body to maximize the blood supply to the brain.

Sometimes, cats are involved in road accidents but still manage to get home. I[f] your cat arrives home in a distressed state, there are some common indication[s] which may suggest that this is what has happened, such as oil and dirt on his coat, broken or split claws, bleeding, ha[ir] loss, distressed breathing, pale gums, or broken limbs – these are just some of th[e] signs. Keep the cat warm and still and rush him to the vet.

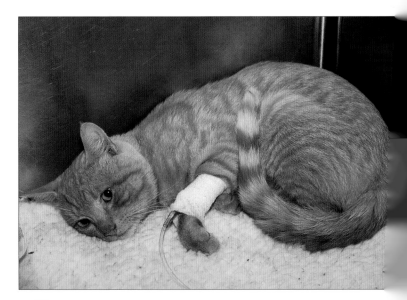

Cats are great climbers and have
extremely good sense of balance, but
their love of high vantage points
ch occasionally lands them in
ble. Fractures of the jaw and limbs
the most common injuries caused by
but less obvious internal injuries
also occur. If you see your cat fall
land awkwardly, or if you suspect
y due to a fall, seek veterinary
tion at once.

oning There are many different
tances to be found around the house
garden which are poisonous to cats.
ever, cats are usually particular
t what they eat and cases of
oning are thankfully rare. The most
mon situation is when a cat eats a
nt which has itself eaten poison,
the effect on the cat will be most
re leading to coma and even death.
ult your vet immediately if you
ect this. Other substances, such as
ehold medicines, can also be
erous and it is important that you
r administer to cats medicines or
ments prescribed for human beings.
en chemicals are also a hazard and
in houseplants are also poisonous if
.

k Your cat could enter a state of
k for a variety of reasons, including

poisoning, heatstroke or as a result of an accident when he will appear weak and cold to the touch and his gums may be a pale greyish colour. Keep him warm by wrapping him loosely in a blanket and call the vet at once.

Fractures   If your cat is in severe pain and is loath to put weight on a leg, he may have broken it. It is most important to keep him as still and as quiet as possible as movement will cause more pain and damage. Lift him up gently, supporting the body but letting the damaged leg dangle. Consult the vet immediately. Do not attempt to make a splint for the injured limb – you could do even more damage. If you suspect a spinal injury, call the vet out to you.

TREATING WOUNDS

Minor Wounds   Clip the hair surrounding the wound, cleaning it thoroughly and treating it with an antiseptic. Consult the vet if you are at all anxious.

Deep Wounds   If your cat has a serious cut which is exposing underlying tissue and bleeding profusely, and if the area can be bandaged, cover it with a thick pad of clean gauze, wrapping a bandage tightly around it to stem the blood flow. If the wound cannot be bandaged, hold the gauze over the wound and apply pressure. Do not apply a tourniquet, you could do even more damage. Rush the cat to the vet.

Arm yourself with a first aid kit for dressing minor wounds, etc.

UNCONSCIOUSNESS AND LOSS OF HEARTBEAT

Check first to establish that the cat is alive. Place him on his side, clear his airway and bring his tongue forward. Establish if there are any broken bones and if so call the vet; if not, you may carefully pick him up and take him to the vet. If there are no signs of life (the cat is not breathing and has no heartbeat), administer cardio-pulmonary resuscitation (CPR).

CARDIO-PULMONARY RESUSCITATION (CPR)

This is a combination of mouth-to-nose resuscitation and cardiac massage.

1. First remove any mucus or obstruction from the mouth or airway, pulling the tongue forward. Place your mouth over the cat's nose and breathe steadily into it for 2–3 seconds, waiting another 2–3 seconds for air to be expelled from the lungs.

2. If the cat fails to resume breathing and/or there is no heartbeat, you will need to apply cardiac massage. Place your hands on the chest just behind the elbow and press down firmly five times with a 1-second interval. Next, repeat the mouth-to-nose sequence, repeating it for 10 minutes or until the heart starts beating again.

3. Once the heart has restarted, cease cardiac massage but carry on with the mouth-to-nose resuscitation until the cat is breathing normally. This could take up to an hour. While you are proceeding with this, ask another person to call the vet for you.

438

BREEDING

Breeding from your own cat is not something which should be entered into lightly. There are already many thousands of unwanted cats in rehoming centres, desperate for kind, loving homes, so producing even more is merely contributing to an already overwhelming problem.

Do not initiate the breeding process until you have firm homes for any kittens which may result, and remember that you, as a breeder, are morally responsible for keeping charge of them in the event of them being rejected by their new owners. Be aware also that it is far more difficult to rehome a non-pedigree than a pedigree cat, so breeding from a non-pedigree cat is definitely a labour of love and can never be for commercial gain.

Breeding pedigree cats is a different matter and breeders pride themselves on their cats' bloodlines, showing them off at cat shows and in magazines where the kittens are often advertised. Once again, don't expect to make a living from this; once stud fees, special dietary requirements for the mother and kittens, as well as registration fees, transfer fees, insurance and vaccinations have been paid for, you will be lucky to break even.

Breeders who produce pedigree cats usually concentrate on a particular breed to which they are devoted, e.g. Siamese.

However, reputable breeders would not encourage novices to breed from their own cats as they are only too aware of the pitfalls of passing on undesirable hereditary traits to future generations, and weakening the breed: you may find that when you buy a kitten it has already been placed on a non-active breeding register, meaning that you will not be able to register any of its offspring.

If you are determined to go ahead, and after carefully weighing up all the advantages and disadvantages, you will proceed to carefully plan the pregnancy.

Never allow your cat to have kittens unless you are confident that you can find homes for every one of them.

439

RIGHT
*Cats usually make
excellent mothers and in
the first few weeks will
care for their kittens
singlehandedly until they
are old enough to
commence solid foods.*

OPPOSITE
*This charming tabby
kitten is alert and aware
of his surroundings – a
sure sign of good health.*

PREGNANCY AND KITTENING

Remember that you should never allow a female which is under a year old to become pregnant. It is assumed that you have done some research to find the perfect mate for your cat in the form of contacting the relevant society for your breed to discover reputable stud owners. Make sure that any potential mate is not related to your cat, as this is a sure way to pass on hereditary defects.

The stud owner will require your female to live in for at least a week and will ask you to supply vaccination and pedigree registration certificates; he will also check that your cat is registered for breeding. These are just some of the requirements before mating can take place.

Once the stud owner is satisfied that everything is in order, he will record all your details and provisionally book your female in. This is the time to make known any of your cat's dietary preferences.

As soon as your female comes into season and begins to call, phone the stud immediately and they will advise you when to bring her in. The stud owner will then keep a careful record of any mating which takes place and when be considers that it has been successful you may take your cat home.

The gestation period for a queen is days; after three weeks her nipples will begin to swell, which is a sure sign that she is pregnant. At this stage, take her

the vet, who will recommend a special diet along with vitamin and mineral supplements. For the rest of her pregnancy you should give her the best possible care and once delivery seems imminent a nesting box in a quiet corner should be provided in which her kittens will be born. You may wish your vet to be present at the birth if you are at all anxious.

Care of the Kittens
It is more than likely that your cat will prove an excellent mother, taking sole charge of her kittens for the first few weeks, keeping them clean and feeding them herself. It is a good idea to keep the family in a confined area as the kittens will soon be on the move and eager to explore.

At around 5 weeks old, you should start to introduce them to solid food such as chicken and fish, offering tiny quantities at first, then at 6 weeks offer ready-prepared canned kitten food. At 9–12 weeks the kittens will be ready for their first vaccinations before going to the new homes you will have already found for them.

If this is the first and only time you are intending to breed from your cat, a good idea to have her neutered, when the risk of further pregnancies will be removed forever.